WHAT DOES GOD WANT?

ALIGNING YOUR LIFE WITH GOD'S DESIRE

SAMUEL WHITEFIELD

What Does God Want? Aligning Your Life with God's Desire
By Samuel Whitefield

Published by OneKing Publishing
PO Box 375
Grandview, MO 64030

Email: contact@oneking.global
Web: https://oneking.global

Copyright © 2020 by OneKing, Inc.
All rights reserved.
ISBN: 978-1-7353454-6-8
eBook ISBN: 978-1-7353454-7-5
This book or any parts of this book may not be reproduced in any form, stored in a retrieval system, or transmitted in any form by any means—electronic, mechanical, photocopy, recording, or otherwise—without the prior permission of the publisher, except as provided by United States of America copyright law.

Unless otherwise noted, all Scripture quotations taken from The Holy Bible, English Standard Version® (ESV®), copyright © 2001 by Crossway, a publishing ministry of Good News Publishers. Used by permission. All rights reserved.

Scripture quotations marked (NASB95) are taken from the New American Standard Bible®, Copyright © 1960, 1962, 1963, 1968, 1971, 1972, 1973, 1975, 1977, 1995 by The Lockman Foundation. Used by permission. www.Lockman.org.

Dedicated to the local church—the crucible the Lord has established to form a people for Himself.

Table of Contents

Introduction 1

What Does God Want?
God's Primary Purpose for This Age 4
God's Burning Desire 14
Will You Answer the Divine Invitation? 28
The Revelation of God Produces a People 34
He Must Be Revealed 46
A Life of Wisdom 56

Will You Respond to Divine Desire?
Jesus' Great Prayer 66
A People with Jesus' Glory 76
Implications of John 17 86
I Want a People 94
God's Undeniable Witness in This Age........................100
Finishing the Task 106
The Revelation of the Mystery 116
Recreating Humanity 126
Instructing the Powers 134
Fuel for Apostolic Labor 142

The Most Neglected End-Time Theme
A Bride like Her Groom 148
The Father's Dream 162

The Revelation of Jesus and His People 170
A Present Demonstration of a Future Reality 184
Do We Share God's Zeal? 192
Acknowledgments 198

INTRODUCTION

What does God want out of this age?

This is the foundational question every human must ask if we want to live with wisdom. However, we tend to live relatively self-focused lives, assuming we know the answer. We assume God wants a "nice" people who live according to a certain moral code. While there are elements of truth in this, it does not accurately reflect God's agenda for this age.

We must know what God wants so that we can cooperate with Him and live a life of wisdom. The biblical term for orienting our lives to God's purposes is *discipleship*. Much of our discipleship is aimless because we do not really know God's purpose for this age. As a result, we reduce discipleship to teaching people new information, trying to get them to follow some rules, and encouraging them toward new habits. Each of these can be valuable tools, but none of them is the essence of discipleship.

Discipleship is a process that reshapes us around God's grand plan for the age. Once you understand His plan, it completely reorients the way you live.

Until we fully know God's purpose for this age, we cannot disciple people correctly, and discipleship is the primary task we have been given.

Jesus commanded us to make disciples, and yet discipleship is often neglected. We neglect it either through lack of involvement, or we reduce it to something much easier and more manageable. If you are not actively engaged in biblical discipleship, though, you are not contributing to the church the way God intends. You may be creating a lot of activity, but you are not really relevant to His great purpose for this age.

Discipleship is hard work, and it can be exhausting, but when you discover God's purpose for this age, discipleship becomes exhilarating!

It takes us into realms of revelation, relationship, and pleasure that we cannot experience any other way.

THE CENTRALITY OF DISCIPLESHIP

The Great Command given by Jesus is to *make disciples:*

> *Go therefore and make disciples of all nations, baptizing them in the name of the Father and of the Son and of the Holy Spirit. (Matthew 28:19)*

Discipleship is the primary task Jesus gave the church in this age, but how much of our time and attention are spent on making disciples? How many of us see this as a noble calling—a great glory?

Discipleship is the main task of the church, but it is often overlooked. For example, there are nearly two billion people who have never heard the gospel,[1] but if we make an incredible effort, it is possible we could carry the gospel to all people within a generation. As a result, many people are talking about "finishing the task" of missions. Still others believe the task can be finished if every person has access to the gospel, but this is not the finish line Jesus gave us. He wants *disciples* in all nations.

There are many people who have a zeal for missions but no vision for discipleship. This is not true missions because the task of missions centers on discipleship. If we evangelize but do not disciple, we have not "finished the task" Jesus gave us.

We must recover a biblical view of the task given to the church if we want to see the task of world missions finished within a generation. Discipleship is the primary task given to the church in this age.

We often reduce discipleship to education or information, but that is not the main point of discipleship. Disciples followed a rabbi and learned his manner of life. Discipleship is not about *information*; it is about *imitation*. Discipleship is often described as a set of behaviors, but that is also not the foundation of discipleship. There are many ways to change people's behavior. Changing behavior does not require Christianity.

---

[1] Patrick Johnstone, *The Future of the Global Church* (Downers Grove: InterVarsity Press, 2014), 161.

Biblical discipleship is much bigger than behavior modification. Spiritual disciplines can be helpful tools, but they are not the goal.

WHAT ARE YOU BUILDING?
Everything should be done with the end in mind.

Discipleship begins with clarity on what God wants out of the age. Once we know what He wants, we can partner with Him. Many of us are trying to live more moral lives while completely out of touch with God's design for the age and the role we play in His plan to obtain a people. As a result, we may pursue a more moral lifestyle, but we are still being carried along by the current of this age.

Can you imagine the shock and pain so many will experience when they realize they did not live with God's purposes for the age in mind?

Jesus warned us not to start a project until we fully calculate the costs of that project.[2] We cannot fully cooperate with God if we do not know what He is building and what it will take. Thankfully, God has revealed His plans plainly in Scripture. Once we see them, we can reorder our lives around them.

This book is part of a series on discipleship. There are many helpful, practical books on discipleship, and readers may find these resources helpful as they pursue a life of discipleship. This series, however, does not seek to duplicate other helpful resources but to make plain the biblical paradigm for discipleship.

"How" we do something is very important, but "why" we do it is even more important. If we do the "how" without the "why," we are in danger of becoming a legalistic people who follow certain rules but are out of touch with the true reason for those rules. In many cases, our discipleship has become focused on the "how" but lost sight of the "why." In this book, we will establish the "why" for this age so we can disciple with clarity.

THE MOST NEGLECTED END-TIME THEME
God's revelation of Himself through Jesus is the most shocking thing He has ever done. However, He is going to do something else that will be the *second most* shocking thing He has ever done. Very few are anticipating it, but it is clearly predicted in the Scripture, and it

---

[2] Luke 14:26–32.

motivated the apostles' labor. It will happen at the end of the age, just before Jesus returns.

God is going to reveal Himself through a people in a stunning way. The closest comparison to what is coming is what God did in Jesus.

This revelation will happen just before the return of Jesus, and it will be shocking and unexpected, just as Jesus' first coming was. There have been glimpses of this throughout history in the church, but something is coming we cannot imagine. Many people have given significant time to studying other end-time signs, but this may well be the most neglected end-time theme in the Bible.

We have spent more time studying the beast (antichrist), the great tribulation, and other details.[3] *However, the Bible is much more focused on the end-time revelation of Jesus' people than these other end-time subjects.*

Even the spiritual powers are going to be shocked and amazed by what God will do,[4] yet most of the church is unaware of what God has in mind.

If we do not understand what God has in mind for the end of the age, we cannot disciple properly.

This book is one in a series on the foundations of discipleship. It examines the essential question: *What does God want, and why did He design this age?*

We'll begin with Paul's longing for the church to know God's purpose so we can live with wisdom and intentionality. I can only imagine how burdened Paul would be for millions of believers who live without this wisdom. Then we will see where Paul got his revelation of God's wisdom and discover Jesus' prayer just before His execution is a profound prophecy about the future of the end-time church. This prophecy is so important the apostles literally gave their lives and suffered to see this prophecy come to pass.

Jesus' prayer and prophecy must drive our labor and focus as it did for the apostles.

We will finish by seeing how much New Testament theology was formed by this single prayer and then examine the Bible's description

---

[3] These subjects must also be carefully studied. The issue is whether we emphasize what the Bible emphasizes.

[4] Ephesians 3:10.

of God's majestic end-time answer to Jesus' prayer: the formation of a people who are like Him. When we realize what the Bible says about God's end-time answer to Jesus' prayer, it gives us the vision we need to embrace our own discipleship *and* to disciple others biblically.

Are you ready to align your life with God's burning desire?

What Does God Want?

GOD'S PRIMARY PURPOSE FOR THIS AGE

This age is not out of control, and it is not meaningless. It is not defined by the purposes of men or the desires of evil powers. God is directing history toward very specific ends that He predetermined before the age began.[1] While evil has created incredible trauma and disfigured God's creation, it has not sidetracked God's agenda. Even the fall of man and the ensuing rebellion of this age serve God's purposes and move His agenda forward.

Discipleship is not primarily about information, rules, and discipline. These things can be helpful tools, but they are not the main focus. The main focus of discipleship is cooperating with God in His agenda for this age, so we cannot make disciples properly if we do not understand His intent.

A lot of energy and activity is being wasted in the church because people do not know the primary purpose of their time in this age.

God has designed this age for two specific purposes.

1. This age exists to reveal God in a way He has not been known before through the person of Jesus.
2. This age exists to form a people for God who have been transformed into His image.

When these purposes are accomplished, the age will end, and time will transition to the next age. *These two purposes are deeply connected, and God has designed everything in this age to accomplish these two purposes. If you intentionally shape your life according to these two purposes, you will live a life of wisdom.*

---

[1] Matthew 25:34; John 17:24; Ephesians 1:4; 1 Peter 1:19–20; Revelation 13:8; 17:8.

If we understand these two purposes, we can fully cooperate with God. If we do not understand them, we will be frustrated in this life as we try to pursue other agendas that are secondary or irrelevant. Millions of well-intentioned people are wasting effort and evaluating their lives incorrectly because they are not aligned with these two purposes.

Far too many Christians do not understand the purpose for this age and, as a result, live out of sync with God's purposes.

Many Christians never consider what the purpose of this age is, and they live relatively aimless lives following whatever their culture's definition of meaning and purpose. They may live according to biblical morality, but these believers lack intentional focus in their lives and spend a lot of energy on entertainment and leisure. Many other believers assume they know the purpose of the age, but their assumptions are not biblical. These Christians are very motivated, but they define success the wrong way and often spend their energy pursuing notoriety, influence, wealth, or comfort.

God's plan in this age is dramatic and multifaceted, but it all revolves around these two purposes. If your life is not primarily oriented around these two purposes, you need to bring your life back into alignment with His goals.

This entire age is God's "immersive classroom,"[2] and we are all in His "school." Imagine diligently doing all your homework for an English class and arriving to school confident and prepared only to discover you have a Math class, not an English one. Many people are engaging in the "classroom" of this age but are studying the wrong "subjects." God wants to help us.

THE IMMERSIVE CLASSROOM

We tend to think of learning as an activity that happens in a formal classroom or an intentional mentorship, but every aspect of our lives is a context for learning. God has carefully designed this age to accomplish His purposes, and once we consider our lives with His ways and His purposes in mind, it will transform the way we approach our daily lives.

Biblical discipleship must be done with God's purposes for the age in mind.

---

[2] A phrase developed by Stuart Greaves in numerous teachings.

God's two purposes for this age both revolve around the knowledge of God, which means discipleship must begin with the knowledge of God. This may seem obvious, but it raises a question: *Do our discipleship programs revolve around the knowledge of God?*

The knowledge of God is something different than mere information about Him. It is possible to know a great amount of information about God while not really knowing Him. You can know intimate details about a person's life, meet him in person, and still be a stranger to him. For example, people can access a lot of information about celebrities yet not know them.

Discipleship is not primarily about information, because it is easy to acquire new information and not change the way you live. Jesus commissioned us to teach people to *observe* His commands, not *learn* them.[3] Of course, we must learn them to observe them, but the goal is a change in the way we live.

Discipleship is about growing in *imitation,* not merely growing in *information.* Many people want to be "students" and not "disciples." Students learn information and repeat it. Disciples imitate. They live with a person and live like that person. They do not just repeat a person's ideas; they adopt the person's lifestyle.

Discipleship is also not primarily about morality. Many systems, philosophies, and religions can help you change your behavior, develop good habits, and change sinful patterns. Many people maintain "good morals" but do not know God. Moral living is a result of discipleship, but discipleship is much more than a path to morality.

When our discipleship programs produce people who are informed about God but do not truly know Him, we set those disciples up for hypocrisy.

The knowledge of God is a relational intimacy with God developed by a certain manner of life with God and His people. There are things about God you can learn in a book, but God has designed this age as His "immersive classroom" to teach you the knowledge of Him. When we think about learning, we tend to focus on information, facts, and data, but this is not the main way God communicates who He is.

The Bible is largely a book of stories because God reveals Himself relationally.

---

[3]Matthew 28:19.

7 What Does God Want?

Sunday sermons are important and helpful, but they are not the primary place where you learn the knowledge of God. You find Him in your joys, your sufferings, your disappointments, your successes, and your failures. Life in this age is designed to reveal God, but we often do not perceive this.

When we ask God to reveal Himself, we expect a new piece of information, but God typically reveals Himself by immersing us into situations that allow us to know Him, identify with Him, and discover Him in ways we never imagined. We seek information, but He gives us experience.

Your deepest joys in life give you insight into God because righteous pleasures are given by God and related to the pleasure He experiences in Himself. When your heart is filled with delight, it should bring you into the heart of God to discover the pleasures in His heart. Your deepest pain will also escort you into new levels of intimacy with God if you will allow it to. Emotional pain, particularly the kind that comes in broken and strained relationships, is probably the most overlooked classroom in God's cosmic university.

God has endured more pain than anyone else, and if you want to know God, you must know His pain. If you *really* want to know Him, He will probably allow you to experience deep pain in one or more of your relationships. When pain comes, we desperately seek immediate relief, but the next time you experience relational pain, perhaps it is an invitation to a deeper knowledge of God.[4]

God has been betrayed, rejected, and mistreated. One of God's most trusted creatures (Satan) corrupted God's prized possession (man), whom God made for Himself as a wife is made for a husband. When God became a man to secure the love of this "wife," she proceeded to betray, torture, and murder Him.

He knows your pain, and He wants you to know His.

Pain is where the most intimate relationships are forged. Your deepest friends are the ones you share your pain with and the ones who share their deepest pains with you. When there is true intimacy, we share the other person's suffering and experience pain in their pain. If you long for the knowledge of God, you will probably experience

---

[4] I am speaking of the relational pain that comes from human brokenness, not the trauma of true abuse. While God was abused and reveals Himself to the abused, this does not mean a person should passively endure abuse and not reach for help.

some deep disappointments that are intended to bring you into the heart of God in ways you never anticipated.

Many people want to experience God's love and share His joy—who will experience His pain?

You can find pleasure in reading a story about the joys of romance and marriage, but it does not compare to the ecstasy of marrying the love of your life, consummating the marriage, and establishing a home together. You can feel a measure of despair watching a movie about betrayal, but a movie is typically resolved in a few hours. It is nothing like the pain of an unexpected betrayal.

If you want the knowledge of God, it will be found in the components of life. Seemingly ordinary experiences will escort you into the heart of God if you will learn God's ways.

God is much more intimate than we think. We have been poisoned by the idea that God is "distant," so we do not realize just how close He is. In truth, He is so close we often miss Him. We look for Him in dramatic and spectacular moments, but this is only one reflection of His nature. When God became a human, He spent at least 90 percent of His life in the ordinary and obscure because He wanted to. He enjoys the ordinary, mundane, and familiar.

- The love of a bride and a bridegroom is a glimpse into the storm of passion in God's soul.
- The joy of a newborn infant is a glimpse into the joy of God in His creation.
- The satisfaction found in diligent work is a picture of God's delight in His management of creation.
- The agony of betrayal is a whisper of what God has suffered from a majestic angel, His prize creation, and what He continues to experience.
- The burden of caring for others is a small expression of God's unceasing task of upholding His creation.
- The pain of suffering and the tragedy of death are a window into God's own pathos over His creation.

If we despise the things of everyday life, we scorn the things God has ordained for our instruction.

9 What Does God Want?

It is utterly tragic that so many people go through life never grasping the purpose for all that they experience.

Most people view life through an intensely personal lens. We are incredibly myopic. As we pass through the events of our lives, we focus on our hopes, our dreams, our fears, and our anxieties. We think about our losses and our gains. We spend all our days and our efforts trying to secure *our* futures. We think life is all about us, but our life experiences are divine classrooms designed to lead us into the discovery of who God is. Furthermore, if we cooperate with the Holy Spirit, not only will we discover God, we will be transformed into His image.

Biblical discipleship will lead people to discover the knowledge of God through active engagement in His immersive classroom.

Setting a Foundation for Discipleship

Your life should be an active pursuit of the knowledge of God as revealed in the person of Jesus. If you have not been captured by the beauty of Jesus, you are out of sync with God's plan for this age.

Because God has designed this age to reveal Himself, there are some questions we must answer as we go:

- Do we know how God reveals Himself in this age?
- Do we know the tools God has given us to discover who He is?
- Do we order our lives around rhythms that lead us into the knowledge of God?

Theological education is important, but we need shepherds who are in full pursuit of the knowledge of God and are fully committed to their own transformation into His image more than we need educated scholars or brilliant orators. Education and gifting are only useful if they are tools in a person's pursuit of the knowledge of God. The process of discipleship shapes and forms people into the image of God, so you cannot disciple people correctly if you do not know God.

God's two purposes for this age—to reveal Himself in a way He has not been known before through the person of Jesus and to form a people for Himself who have been transformed into His image—must determine how we train and select leaders.

Paul had a brilliant mind and could have explored many subjects, but he decided to focus his entire capacity on just one subject: *Christ and Him crucified*:

For I decided to know nothing among you except Jesus Christ and him crucified. (1 Corinthians 2:2)

Paul recognized this age is designed for the revelation of God through the person of Jesus *and* our transformation into His image, so he aligned himself with God's purposes. That alignment reveals Paul's insight into the knowledge of God, which in turn enabled him to become a foundational apostle and instruct others to "follow him." (Paul's decision to know Jesus led him to a life of imitation. When we "limit" ourselves to Jesus, we do not withdraw from His people or our associated responsibilities.)

The apostle Paul may not have been the best preacher in his generation, but he was captured by Jesus[5] and committed to being transformed into Jesus' image even though it cost Him tremendously.[6] Paul's alignment to God's purposes was at the center of his life and the reason he continues to have unparalleled influence in our time.

What could we accomplish if we fully aligned our lives to God's purposes for the age?

Discipleship is a way of living that enables you to discover the knowledge of God and be transformed into His image. There are many tools that can serve this purpose such as education, discipline, and new habits, but those tools cannot become the primary objective of discipleship. To be valuable, every tool must serve this two-fold purpose:

- Help disciples grow in the knowledge of God as revealed in the person of Jesus.
- Transform disciples into the image of Jesus and enable them to become like Him.

---

[5] 1 Corinthians 1:23; 2:2; Galatians 6:14; Philippians 1:23–24.

[6] 1 Corinthians 4:9–13; 2 Corinthians 11:23–27; Philippians 3:8–10; 2 Timothy 4:6.

Is your life oriented around these purposes? If not, it is time to align yourself with God's agenda.

Are you leading others according to these two goals? If not, it is time to reevaluate your approach to discipleship.

What Are We Supposed to Build?

Before a building is built, an architect creates building plans so everyone knows what they are building. There may be surprises and changes in the building process, but the plans keep the project on track and bring unity to the project. If no one knows what the intended outcome of a project is, the project is already a failure.

If God has designed this entire age to produce a companion for His Son, we need to know what the Bible says about that companion. What kind of people is God going to give to His Son? The Bible describes this companion as Jesus' "bride,"[7] and this gives us a glimpse of what God wants. A bride is a beautiful, mature companion prepared and ready to be joined to her husband, and this is the way the Bible describes the end-time church.

Discipleship is the exhausting, glorious, difficult, mundane, and fulfilling task of partnering with the Father to prepare Jesus' reward.

Regardless of what we think about the church, God has fully committed to Jesus that the church is going to be faithful, loyal, passionate, and mature when He returns. The church is God's gift to Jesus in this age, and the Father only gives spectacular gifts to His one and only Son.

Before this age ends, God is going to shock and amaze the nations and the spiritual powers by producing a people who are compatible to Jesus—a people so stunning they will be a fitting reward for His suffering. Jesus has waited thousands of years for this people, and the bride the Father is going to give Jesus will be worth the wait.

The Bible predicts the mature church will be one of the most remarkable end-time signs.

People carefully study several end-time details—and we should study them all—but the revelation of the end-time church is one of the most overlooked end-time signs. The New Testament says much more about the end-time church than the beast (antichrist), but tragically

---

[7]Ephesians 5:22–32; Revelation 19:7–9.

most people probably know more about the rule of the beast than they do the end-time church. This is troubling, but it is also *temporary.*

The apostles labored tirelessly because they knew what the Father had promised Jesus. The age will not end until this people emerge out of the nations,[8] so God is going to give the church the revelation the apostles had. We need fresh eyes to see, *really see*, what the Bible says about Jesus' people. When we see what the apostles understood, we will labor with the same intensity, zeal, and resolve they had.

One of our greatest challenges is a low view of the church. The New Testament does not ignore the challenges of the local church, but it also has a much higher view of the church than most believers do. The authors were confident God is going to form a people like Jesus, and they described the future of the church in language that is almost foreign in our time. They stated the church would be made in Jesus' image and receive a glorious body like His.[9] As we begin our study, we need two firm convictions that enable us to avoid unbiblical ideas: We will never become God, and we will never be worshipped. With these two firm convictions, we need to understand what the Bible says about the glory of the church. It will go far beyond what most people imagine.

---

[8] Acts 1:6–8; Revelation 5:9; 7:9.

[9] Romans 8:29; 1 Corinthians 15:49; 2 Corinthians 3:18; 4:10–11; 1 John 3:2.

GOD'S BURNING DESIRE

Creation was not made for a function; it was birthed out of desire.

Colossians 1 contains one of Paul's grand descriptions of Jesus' majesty. In the passage, Paul revealed God's purpose for His creation and His people. Paul also answered the existential questions humans ask, and his answer is spectacular.

Paul considered the information in this chapter so important that he and his team prayed unceasingly for the Colossians:

> *And so, from the day we heard, we have not ceased to pray for you, asking that you may be filled with the knowledge of his will in all spiritual wisdom and understanding. (Colossians 1:9)*

The Colossians were obviously important to Paul because he had begun praying for them as soon as he heard of their faith.[1] In fact, this was the second time in six verses Paul had told them he prayed constantly for them.[2] Paul had a practice of constant prayer for his coworkers, friends, and the churches he knew,[3] so this was not unusual, but Paul had a specific burden that fueled his ongoing prayer for this church.

Paul did not establish the church in Colossae, so he did not have the chance to lay foundations he typically laid when he formed a new church. He prayed constantly for the Colossians because he wanted them to know these foundations. Paul also summarized these

---

[1] Colossians 1:3–8.

[2] Colossians 1:3, 9.

[3] Romans 1:9–10; Ephesians 1:16–23; Philippians 1:3–5; Colossians 1:3, 9–12; 1 Thessalonians 5:15–18; 2 Thessalonians 1:3.

15 WHAT DOES GOD WANT?

foundations in his letter, and it gives us a glimpse into his church planting.

Paul's burden and his prayer were very specific. He prayed the church would be "filled with the knowledge of God's will in all spiritual wisdom and understanding." The word *will* (θέλημα) carries a sense of desire, and Paul's prayer can be translated this way: "We are constantly praying for you, asking God that you would fully know God's desire so you can live with wisdom and understanding."

God's will expresses His longing—His own deep desires. It is not simply a set of rules or an expected pattern of behavior. His deep desire gave birth to the cosmos. If we understand that desire, we can live with wisdom. If we do not know His desire, we will live out of sync with Him, even if we belong to Jesus.

Paul wanted the church to fully know God's desires so she could live in response to divine desire with wisdom and understanding.

Paul's discovery of God's divine desire radically reoriented his life, and he wanted the same revelation for the Colossians because he knew it would produce specific fruit in their lives:

> *Walk in a manner worthy of the Lord, fully pleasing to him: bearing fruit in every good work and increasing in the knowledge of God; being strengthened with all power, according to his glorious might, for all endurance and patience with joy; giving thanks to the Father, who has qualified you to share in the inheritance of the saints in light. (Colossians 1:10–12)*

The revelation of God's desire is so powerful, it radically transforms our lives. Paul prayed the knowledge of God's will would produce at least seven responses in the Colossians:

1. Walk in a manner worthy of the Lord—This was a phrase Paul commonly used[4] to describe a way of life in alignment with God's purposes, including what He has done, what He is doing, and what He will do.

2. Be fully pleasing to the Lord—When we live in alignment with God and order our lives around His purposes, we can *fully* please Him. Paul knew, if the church was ignorant of God's

---

[4]Ephesians 4:1; Philippians 1:27; Colossians 1:10; 1 Thessalonians 2:12.

plan, the church could genuinely love Him, but not be aligned with His purposes. Paul did not want the Colossians to experience the pain and loss of a life out of sync with God.

3. Bear fruit in every good work—Insight into God's will would enable the Colossians to bear incredible fruit because their labor would be aligned with God's desire.

4. Increase in the knowledge of God—Understanding God's desires leads us into the knowledge of God. As we learn what He deeply wants, we discover who He is.

5. Be strengthened with all power according to His glorious might—When the Colossians grasped God's purposes and lived in sync with them, they would receive incredible strength and power. God's desires are backed by His own incredible might. When we live in sync with Him, His power works on our behalf.

6. Endurance and patience with joy—Knowledge of God gives us the ability to patiently endure difficulties with joy.

7. Give thanks to the Father—Knowing God's will would cause the Colossians to erupt in praise and gratitude as they realized the inheritance they had been given when they became part of the church.

Paul prayed earnestly for this church because there are serious consequences when God's people are not filled with the knowledge of His will. Paul's prayer implies that, if a church does not grasp the desire of God, it will:

- Live beneath God's calling for His people.
- Not fully please Him (out of ignorance not rebellion).
- Miss out on good works and bear less fruit.
- Have an incomplete knowledge of God.
- Lack strength to live according to God's purposes.
- Lack endurance, patience, and joy.
- Lack gratitude and thankfulness.

17 What Does God Want?

When we think about God's "will," we tend to think about specific decisions we need to make or moral boundaries God has established. These things are part of His will, but Paul had something bigger in mind. Paul wanted to give the Colossians a new paradigm, a framework for reality. God's will in individual decisions is important, but the Colossians needed to know why God created the cosmos and why He created them.

When you know God's cosmic purposes and His desire for this age, it becomes much easier to navigate situations and make decisions that are fully pleasing to God.

Many people are anxious about making decisions and seek the Lord for insight, but the answer does not always come by fixating on an individual decision. There are times God gives specific guidance for certain decisions, but in most cases He wants us to make decisions that align us with His overarching purposes. (And many times there is not one specific decision that is best. Often the Lord gives us a choice between more than one option that will accomplish His purposes.)

Clearly, we *must* know God's will for His creation, so what is this divine desire that gave birth to the cosmos and continues to drive God's purpose for what He has made? Thankfully, it is not a mystery. Paul summarized God's will right after his prayer so the Colossians would know what He was praying for them.

After his introduction, Paul launched into one of the most majestic and dense passages ever written by a human being. Every phrase he recorded is filled with revelation:

> *He is the image of the invisible God, the firstborn of all creation. For by him all things were created, in heaven and on earth, visible and invisible, whether thrones or dominions or rulers or authorities—all things were created through him and for him. And he is before all things, and in him all things hold together. . . . For in him all the fullness of God was pleased to dwell. (Colossians 1:15–17, 19)*

As Paul described the grandeur of Jesus, he summarized the driving impetus of God's will: *"All things were created through him and for him."* This phrase unveils the burning desire of God that gave birth to the cosmos and drives His will for His creation and His people. We need to be filled with the knowledge of what this phrase means.

THE COSMOS IS A STAGE

Everything that exists—including heaven, Earth, visible, invisible, spiritual beings, evil spiritual powers, and humanity—was all made *by* Jesus and made *for* Jesus. Every single thing in the cosmos—whether good or evil, material or spiritual—has been made for Him.

This age, the cosmos, and everything in it are a stage that God set for Jesus.

Paul reveals something deep in the heart of God: *God has a burning desire to be known.* God does not want to dwell alone. His desire to be known is so strong it gave birth to the entire cosmos and all of history.

Creation was not formed out of God's need. It was made from God's desire.

God dwelled in complete and total perfection in eternity past. He lacked nothing. He existed in relationship with Himself as the triune God, and yet He was unknown because no other creature existed to know Him. However, He was not content dwelling alone in perfection. He had a burning desire to be known and loved, so a plan was formed. God designed the cosmos as His stage, a stage He could step on and a context filled with creatures who could finally see who He really is.

God began with the spiritual powers and the heavenly realm. He fashioned a throne in the heavenly realm, and the descriptions of this throne are vivid and terrifying.[5] Seated on His heavenly throne, God could be seen in the heavens as the majestic unequaled Creator, but His glory obscured the deepest parts of His nature. His majesty was on full display, but He dwelled in unapproachable light:

> *He who is the blessed and only Sovereign, the King of kings and Lord of lords, who alone has immortality, who dwells in unapproachable light, whom no one has ever seen or can see. To him be honor and eternal dominion. Amen. (1 Timothy 6:15–16)*

God's glory filled the heavens, but He had a profound dilemma. The light of His glory both revealed *and* covered Him. God wanted to be known *as He is*, but His being is so majestic no one could really see Him. He was known yet unknown as the glory of His being was on display yet obscured the full revelation of who He was. The heavenly realm expressed God's desire, but He wanted a context where He could

---

[5] Isaiah 6:1–7; Revelation 4–5.

19 WHAT DOES GOD WANT?

be known *intimately*—a place where His creation could see who He truly is. This desire gave birth to the cosmos.

God created the cosmos and filled it with creatures. He finished by making a creature called *man*.[6] This creature was more humble and lowly than many other spiritual beings, yet this creature was made as God's image. God chose this lowly creature for a very specific purpose: to make Himself known and to become His most intimate companion.

God's choice of a humble, earthy creature as His image and His companion carried a profound message: God is humble and lowly. He is attracted to humility and delights in lowliness.[7]

When God made man, He already had "sons of God" in the heavenly realm,[8] but they did not have the lowliness necessary to reveal God and become His companion. The heavenly powers[9] displayed dimensions of God's glory, but God could not take their form because the spiritual powers did not carry the lowliness necessary to fully reveal God.[10] The lack of lowliness also meant they could not relate to God as His most intimate companion.

God made man to reveal who He is. He made man as His "image" and the creature He would become. Because God is humble, He shaped a humble creature capable of revealing His own nature.

God could have dwelled in absolute perfection in eternity, but He wanted to be known, so He formed creation as His stage, and this age as His first act. This entire age is designed to reveal aspects of God that would otherwise remain hidden. This is God's first purpose for

---

[6] Genesis 1–2.

[7] Psalm 138:6; Proverbs 3:34; 15:33; 18:12; 22:4; Isaiah 57:15; Matthew 23:12; 1 Peter 5:5; James 4:6.

[8] Job 1:6; 2:1; 38:7.

[9] We typically refer to these as *angels*, but that word indicates a function. The Bible refers to these beings as *elohim*, indicating they are powerful spiritual beings.

[10] If Satan was in fact a majestic angel, it is possible his fall began with envy when he discovered God's desire to reveal His glory in another creature. The angels could bear a measure of the majesty of God, as evidenced by the fear most men feel when they encounter them, but the angels did not have the humility necessary to fully reveal God.

creation and for this age. This is His will, and if we do not know it, we will not live in agreement with His purposes.

GOD STEPPED ON HIS OWN STAGE

God always intended to become part of His creation so He could be known, but His plan was a mystery for centuries. God formed and shaped His stage for thousands of years, and then He suddenly stepped on the stage and revealed His shocking plan: *He would fully reveal Himself in the Man Jesus.*

This entire age and everything in it are part of God's glorious stage. This includes the spiritual realm, the physical creation, every creature that exists, human relationships, and even the nations. *Everything* created was designed to make God known to us.[11]

Jesus is the "firstborn" of creation because it was all formed so He could become man and make God known.

Jesus is the unifying theme of creation—everything comes together in Him.[12] He is both divine and creature, both spiritual and physical, and in that union He reveals the divine nature in a way it could not be revealed if God had not become part of His own creation.

When God sat enthroned in the heavens, His majesty, dominion, and supremacy could be seen, but the deepest aspects of who God is were not known. He had to enter the cosmos to be fully known by His creation. More specifically, God entered the *fallen* cosmos to reveal who He truly is.

God can only be fully known in a fallen cosmos, and this is at the heart of the mystery of God's leadership over the rebellion in this age.

When you read the Bible carefully, you discover a profound mystery: The rebellion has played a part in God's purposes from the very beginning. The rebellion in this age is obviously fueled by opposition to God's will, and yet without the rebellion, God would never have been known the way He wants to be known, nor would He have the companion He wants.

---

[11] Romans 1:20; Colossians 1:16.

[12] Ephesians 1:10; Colossians 1:20.

21 WHAT DOES GOD WANT?

The rebellion has created tremendous devastation, and God is going to judge the perpetrators of evil, but without the rebellion, aspects of God's nature would have remained hidden forever. The rebellion of this age created a perfect stage for the revelation of the depth of who God really is. Before the rebellion, God's majesty was apparent, but the depths of His mercy, humility, and love were not known. Above all, this age is an optimal environment for God to unveil His self-sacrificing nature.

When Jesus was beaten and whipped and finally nailed to a tree that He made, God was suddenly, graphically, and shockingly revealed. It was not an accident that Jesus was stripped naked when He was executed. It was part of God's message to us: *This is Me fully exposed.* As long as He sat in the heavens, God could not be fully seen. He was veiled by the splendor and terror of the glory that surrounds His majestic throne. On the cross, however, God was naked. Fully revealed. In the humiliation of a crucified, human form, God was fully unmasked and no longer obscured by unapproachable light.

God revealed Himself to all of creation on the cross. Humanity saw who God truly is. Even angels, demons, and spiritual powers suddenly saw a revelation of God they had never seen. For thousands of years, the creatures nearest God had been crying out incessantly as they caught glimpses of God's majesty. However, they had never seen anything like what they saw on the cross.

What did the heavenly creatures and the seraphim scream in response when they saw God exposed and revealed on the cross?

"Holy! Holy! Holy!" is the first response the creatures have when they encounter the revelation of God on His throne.[13] *Holy* does not primarily mean morally perfect; it means "completely different from anything else." When the creatures get a glimpse of God, they summarize what they see by saying, *"He is completely different from anything else. We do not have words to describe what we have seen!"*

Because of the heavenly storm that surrounds God's presence,[14] it is easy to assume this cry of *Holy!* is a response to God's power and majesty, but it is much more than that. In Revelation 4–5, John

---

[13] Revelation 4:8.

[14] Ezekiel 1; Revelation 4:5.

describes the heavenly storm and then explains the heavenly creatures' scream in awe because of the *"Slain Lamb"* standing in their midst:

> *And the four living creatures, each of them with six wings, are full of eyes all around and within, and day and night they never cease to say, "Holy, holy, holy, is the Lord God Almighty, who was and is and is to come!" (Revelation 4:8)*

> *And between the throne and the four living creatures and among the elders I saw a Lamb standing, as though it had been slain, with seven horns and with seven eyes, which are the seven spirits of God sent out into all the earth. (5:6)*

Revelation 5:6 is translated slightly differently in various English translations, but it means John saw the Lamb standing in the center of the heavenly beings surrounding the throne.[15] The living creatures are not only responding to the majesty of the "one upon the throne," they are responding to the revelation of God in the Man Jesus *and* His suffering.

Heavenly creatures only cry, "Holy, holy, holy," twice in the Bible. The first time is found in Isaiah's vision in Isaiah 6.[16] In the gospel of John, we discover this vision was a vision of Jesus,[17] and John mentions Isaiah's vision in a passage about a crowd's unbelief about Jesus and His prediction He must suffer. John's decision to reference Isaiah's vision in this passage indicates Isaiah's vision of Jesus also revealed Jesus as the One who would suffer.

Isaiah saw Jesus as the "Slain Lamb," which is why the creatures were screaming, *"Holy, holy, holy!"* We typically use a bold font, an exclamation mark, or large fonts to show emphasis, but ancient authors used repetition to emphasize a word and communicate intensity, shouting, etc. So, this is an indicator the creatures are shouting, "Holy!" as loudly as they can. One scholar has proposed "Holy, holy, holy" is

---

[15] Robert H. Mounce, *The Book of Revelation*, The New International Commentary on the New Testament (Grand Rapids, MI: Wm. B. Eerdmans Publishing Co., 1997), 134.

[16] Isaiah 6:3.

[17] John 12:41.

better translated *"Holy, exceedingly holy!"*[18] In other words, He is completely unlike us. There are no human words capable of describing just who He is.

Isaiah not only recorded the only instance of "Holy, holy, holy" outside of Revelation 4, he also prophesied of Jesus as the "Suffering Servant" and recorded a graphic prophetic description of Jesus' suffering in Isaiah 53. Isaiah even predicted this "Suffering Servant" would be marred more than any other man:

> *Behold, my servant shall act wisely; he shall be high and lifted up, and shall be exalted. As many were astonished at you—his appearance was so marred, beyond human semblance, and his form beyond that of the children of mankind. (Isaiah 52:13–14)*

We do not know exactly what Isaiah saw in Isaiah 6, but whatever he saw shocked him and made him ashamed of the words he had spoken:

> *And I said: "Woe is me! For I am lost; for I am a man of unclean lips, and I dwell in the midst of a people of unclean lips; for my eyes have seen the King, the LORD of hosts!" (v. 5)*

There is no question Jesus' majesty overwhelmed Isaiah,[19] but his response to the vision and his subsequent revelation indicate Isaiah was given a glimpse of the One John described as the "Slain Lamb." Isaiah certainly would have known his predictions of the "Suffering Servant" were related to the One he saw on the throne.

Isaiah's vision of Jesus in Isaiah 6 was directly connected to his revelation of Jesus as a slain lamb in Isaiah 53.

Both times heavenly creatures cry out, *"God is completely different from any other person! We have no words to describe Him!"* (Holy, holy, holy!) It is a response to the revelation of God that has come in the person of Jesus through His suffering in this age. The heavenly creatures are awed by every expression of God's majesty, but the Bible uniquely emphasizes their response to Jesus and Him crucified as the highest revelation of

---

[18] Norman Walker. "The Origin of the 'Thrice-Holy,'" *New Testament Studies* 5, no. 2 (1959): 132–33. doi:10.1017/S0028688500009280.

[19] Isaiah 6:4.

who God truly is and what makes Him completely different from every other creature.

The living creatures cry, "Holy, holy, holy!" because of the revelation of God that has come in the person of Jesus through His suffering in this age.

The apex of the heavenly creatures' response to God's glory occurs when He appears as the suffering God in humility. We are easily awed by God's power, but the cosmos was formed to show who He truly is and what ultimately makes Him holy and unlike any other person. When we think of the height of God's glory, do we think primarily of the One upon the throne surrounded by thunder, lightning, and earthquakes, or do we think of the revelation of God in the suffering of Jesus? We do not need to choose one or the other, but humans are naturally attracted to strength, so it is easy to be awed by God's sheer might. It takes revelation to love and know God in His suffering.

God formed this age so the deepest parts of His person would be revealed. He wanted the entire cosmos to see what makes the creatures cry out, *"Holy! Exceedingly holy!"*

If Jesus had never faced the rebellion in this age, the deepest aspects of who God is would never have been made known. God would have remained partially unknown throughout eternity. He would be feared, worshipped, and perhaps loved but not really known. God wanted to be known so deeply that He willingly chose a path of suffering and humiliation so we could see Him fully exposed.

God willingly chose to hand Himself over to evil powers,[20] knowing that agony served His purposes. He intentionally designed a cosmos that could reveal these hidden parts of His nature. He purposefully exposed Himself in the context of an evil age. While He is not the author of evil or suffering, this age is an intentional and necessary context for God to be known the way He wants to be known.

The exposure of God on the cross is a divine invitation: "Do you want to know Me as I in fact am?"

Paul understood the invitation, so he committed his entire life to one pursuit:

---

[20]Matthew 17:22; 20:18–19; Luke 18:31–33; 24:7; Mark 9:31; 10:33–34.

25 What Does God Want?

> *For I decided to know nothing among you except Jesus Christ and him crucified. (1 Corinthians 2:2)*

We know Paul was given the gospel by revelation, was caught up to the heavenly realm, and had a deep hunger for the knowledge of God.[21] God even chose to humble Paul because of the "surpassing greatness of his revelations."[22] Perhaps Paul saw the heavenly creatures and heard their response to God's beauty. We know that he was given unusual access to the revelation of God, and he decided to limit himself to the same thing that captivated the heavenly creatures: *Jesus and Him crucified.* The question is will we?

Paul discovered what the heavenly creatures also discovered: God is revealed most completely in the person of Jesus and His suffering.[23]

Paul's response is the only worthy response to what Jesus has done. If this entire age exists to make God known and God has made Himself known most completely in the person of Jesus, and more specifically in Jesus' horrific suffering, then the only reasonable response to God's self-revelation is to search out everything God has made known about Himself. God designed this age so we can discover Jesus and Him crucified.

When we do not prioritize the revelation of God in the person of Jesus and His suffering, we are not in line with the purpose of God for this age, and we show a lack of value for God's costly revelation of Himself.

God wanted to be known so badly He became a creature and then endured the most horrific abuse from other creatures—*all so He could be known.* How have you responded to this revelation? Have you oriented your life like Paul? Or do other things still capture your affection? Do your discipleship methods provoke people to orient their lives the way Paul did?

If you are a minister, what is your *real* focus? What drives your effort and stirs your emotions? Is it the success of a "ministry," or like

---

[21] 2 Corinthians 12:2–4; Galatians 1:12, 15–16.

[22] 2 Corinthians 12:7.

[23] Jesus famously cried out, "It is finished" (John 19:30). This cry is obviously full of meaning, but perhaps God's revelation of Himself on the cross is one of the things "finished" in Jesus' suffering.

Paul, are you fixated on the person of Jesus *and* His crucifixion? Tragically, even ministry can quickly become a vehicle for personal ambition, and ministers can function more like executives in a corporation than apostles.[24] When you minister to others, what do you give them? Do you give them a few self-help tools? A few practical disciplines? Or do you convey the knowledge of Jesus and Him crucified to them?[25]

If someone observed your life and then had to summarize the pursuit of your life with one theme, would they say Jesus and Him crucified?

Paul was an impressive church planter and managed a wide network of relationships. He even periodically ran a small business in tents. Yet, he intentionally limited himself to one subject: *Jesus and Him crucified*. If we want Paul's results, we need to follow Paul's path.

Paul's focus on Jesus is what made Paul who he was. If you set yourself to pursue the knowledge of Jesus, you will experience a similar transformation. The knowledge of Jesus crucified is not a collection of information. If you truly pursue the knowledge of the Divine Man, He quickly issues an invitation: *"Do you want to become like Me?"* God's purpose in this age is the revelation of Himself *and* the formation of a people who are like Him.

---

[24]This is a statement about values not necessarily organizational structure.

[25]Disciplines, habits, and tools are valuable if they support the main goal of beholding Jesus and do not become the main goal. For more on this, see the companion book, *Discipleship Begins With Beholding*.

WILL YOU ANSWER THE DIVINE INVITATION?

If you want to live with wisdom, you must live as if God created all things and designed this entire age to reveal Himself in the person of Jesus.

God's revelation of Himself is an invitation. He wants a people to respond and then become like Him. It is possible to be grateful for the forgiveness the cross secured but not realize the cross is a divine invitation to go beyond forgiveness into the revelation of who God is and ultimately become like Him. We can receive the mercy of the atonement and miss the main purpose of the atonement.

Our lack of response to the divine invitation given on the cross is outrageous and perplexing to the angels.

Paul summarized God's will (desire) for the Colossians, but before we continue we need to let this revelation escort us into the ocean of God's desire. The atonement was not just an act of legal forgiveness; it was a vivid demonstration of desire that came from the most emotional Person in the cosmos.

I WANT YOU TO KNOW ME

If you view creation biblically, you should hear God's thunderous voice proclaiming, "I want you to know Me." He formed and shaped everything as a stage to reveal Himself, and His magnificent stage has been severely damaged by sin and rebellion. As a result, many think this age is a "mistake," and they fixate on their own suffering, never considering that *God has suffered more* from the fall of man than any creature. Yet, God chose to set His own suffering into motion because it served His determination to make Himself known in a way He could have never been known in a "perfect" universe.

29 What Does God Want?

Because the cosmos was made to reveal God, He had to become part of the cosmos. In the person of Jesus, He is transcendent, infinitely greater than the created realm, *and* also a part of the created realm. For this reason, He will remake the cosmos but never destroy it because it reveals who He is and He is inseparably bound to it.

He formed creation, sustains creation, and suffers tremendously in His creation, because He wants to reveal and make known what was previously hidden. It is not enough for God to be who He is. He wants to be *known*. He wants to be pursued, searched out, and discovered. He wants a creature to be intimately acquainted with Him. He wants to put the deepest parts of who He is on display.

Do you see the cross as an event, a transaction, or an invitation?

David wrote in Psalm 139:

You search out my path and my lying down and are acquainted with all my ways. Even before a word is on my tongue, behold, O LORD, you know it altogether. You hem me in, behind and before, and lay your hand upon me. Such knowledge is too wonderful for me; it is high; I cannot attain it. . . . My frame was not hidden from you, when I was being made in secret, intricately woven in the depths of the earth. Your eyes saw my unformed substance; in your book were written, every one of them, the days that were formed for me, when as yet there was none of them. How precious to me are your thoughts, O God! How vast is the sum of them! If I would count them, they are more than the sand. I awake, and I am still with you. (vv. 3–6, 15–18)

Do you realize God wants you to interpret His activity in Psalm 139 as an invitation?

God takes great delight in knowing who you are. He sees all your ways. He knows you intimately. He has searched you out. The question is, who will search Him out? Who will seek out the hidden parts of His Person? Yes, He is infinite and the knowledge of who He is can never be exhausted, but who will try? Are you content to read Psalm 139 and bask in God's pursuit of you? Are you satisfied with Him searching you out and knowing you? Is it enough for you to be known? Or do you grasp *His* desire to be known and searched out?

Psalm 139 is an invitation to you to search out the hidden places of the Divine Person.

Animals do not seek to be known by others, but men want someone to desire them and take time to truly know them. *Do you realize this desire is God's desire?* You want to be known because you are made in His image. Men will go to incredible lengths to be loved and known. They will do outlandish things and take incredible risks, hoping someone will love them. As strong as our desire to be known is, it is a weak expression of His desire. His desire to be known drove Him to choose a humiliating execution, knowing that many would never respond.

God searched you out when you were His enemy and resisted Him.[1] Will you search Him out now that He is your Savior, or are you too self-centered? Will you stare at Him exposed and revealed in His crucified Son until you can see past the horror of it all to see the center of the Divine Heart? He wants you to enjoy His love, but He is looking for a people who will find incredible pleasure in searching Him out.

The fullness of who God is dwells in His Son because He is the One God made creation for. In Him you can fully know God. In Him God is reconciling you to *Himself*.[2] Many want to be reconciled to eternal life or obtain some sort of blessing, but do you want to be reconciled *to Him*? Is He the thing you want, or are you searching for another prize?

THE PRICE WAS WORTH IT

Thousands of years. An entire cosmos. Myriads of heavenly beings. Billions of humans. The tragedy of the fall. The pain of seeing and hearing every sin. An excruciating, humiliating death. The ongoing weight of sustaining creation. Constant accusations and the rejection of so many. *This is the price God has paid to be made known in the person of His Son.*

The value of something is shown by the price you are willing to pay. God's desire for a people who will become His companion is demonstrated by what He has endured for thousands of years. People treat God as if He is unaffected by the troubles and pain of the cosmos and removed from what goes on in His creation. However, He

---

[1] Romans 5:8–10.

[2] 2 Corinthians 5:19.

feels the pain of the cosmos most intensely. He demonstrated His pain on the cross—He felt the pain of *His* execution. Nails were driven through His flesh in participation with our suffering. He was disfigured more than any other human.[3] He submitted to the rage of the powers.[4] The cross was a graphic revelation that He suffers with creation in ways we cannot fathom.

When God became a man, He entered into the pain of humanity. His suffering on the cross was a demonstration of what He has felt since the beginning of the rebellion. He bears with His creation night and day as His masterpiece is destroyed over and over. The beauty He formed is continually turned into the most grotesque things.

The cross was not God's only moment of suffering. He chose to endure this fallen age to secure an eternal companion.

The cross was God's gruesome demonstration that He suffers. We are consumed by our own suffering in this fallen age, but what of His suffering? Do you consider the pain He bears? We see one small part of the suffering in this age, but He endures it all. He is the Owner and the Creator of everything, yet He is rejected and maligned more than any other. Everyone wants answers for their suffering, but no one asks Him what He has suffered.

He has suffered the greatest loss.

He has paid a price no creature can fathom to make His Son's glory known and to secure a companion. Consider the price. Every life. Every moment. Every part of the cosmos. It is all part of the price He has paid to secure what He wants.

God would say, *"It's worth it. It's worth it to make my Son known. It's worth it to secure a companion."*

God enjoys dwelling in human flesh. It's not a burden to Him. It's not something He had to do; He willingly decided to dwell in a human body. He was *pleased* to do what He did.[5] We do not grasp His delight in His people. We cannot fathom His joy even in His suffering. No one really grasps the depth of His goodness. He did not agree to become a

---

[3] Isaiah 52:14.

[4] 1 Corinthians 2:8; Hebrews 12:3.

[5] Isaiah 53:10; John 12:24; Hebrews 12:2.

sacrifice under compulsion; *He is self-sacrificing.* He takes deep delight in giving Himself for His creation. We consider it a burden to give our lives for the sake of someone else, but it is not a burden for Him. It is who He is. He naturally gives Himself.

We do not know the depth of His joy. There is nothing we can do to add to His joy. We do not realize how truly glad He is. He is joyful in a way we cannot imagine. We cannot fathom the way He enjoys pouring out His Spirit.

The heart of the divine mystery that Jesus revealed is not a secret plan or hidden information. *God is the mystery* that we cannot discern on our own or fully grasp in our human thinking. So many people are looking for their answers in secret knowledge and hidden information, but if you discover Him, you discover all things. If God had never taken on flesh, there are parts of Him that would never have been known and, furthermore, never could have been known, but those parts have now been revealed.

Jesus is God's mystery. The mystery is that God can dwell in a human body and reveal Himself through suffering in a way that He would never have been known if He had not created a cosmos and chosen to become a creature in it.

God has joined Himself to creation to live in our space as a divine human so we can come into the knowledge of who He is. He spoke about this to the prophets, but it was impossible to comprehend the mystery until He did it. The mystery could not be revealed until He became a part of His creation as a man. The revelation of who He is required an incarnation, and an incarnation required a cosmos. He wanted that cosmos filled with creatures who could enjoy the incarnation with Him. His mystery would have remained a mystery if no one was created to see it, so He formed and fashioned human spectators to see the mystery exposed.

When these spectators gaze on the mystery that is revealed in Jesus, they are invited to become part of the mystery. If they will respond to the invitation, the Spirit will transform them, and they will become a corporate demonstration of the mystery if they continue to gaze at God's mystery revealed in His Son.

God's mystery is revealed in humanity, and that mystery is revealed in a people who have His Spirit. When the Spirit dwells in you, He makes you an image of the Divine Human. You become "like" His

33 What Does God Want?

Son.[6] Though you are limited by your sinful flesh, you still reveal His Mystery.

God carefully constructed everything in this age, including the angels, the beings that rebelled, the earth, humanity, *everything*, so we could know Him and become like Him.

This age is God's great invitation to you, "Do you want to really know Me? And become like Me?"

---

[6]See Romans 8:29; 1 Corinthians 15:49; 2 Corinthians 3:18; Ephesians 4:24; Philippians 3:21. Though obviously there are limitations, we have not truly grasped what the Bible says.

The Revelation of God Produces a People

God's burning desire to be known begins with the revelation of Himself, but it does not stop there. God has revealed Himself so He can be known by a people who search Him out and in the process become like Him. God's revelation of Himself is producing a people who will be compatible to Him.

The goal of discipleship is to become like God; therefore, it must begin with beholding God—encountering the revelation of God in the person of Jesus.

As we have seen, when Paul summarized the will of God, He began with the idea that all of creation is a stage fashioned by God to make His Son known:

> *He is the image of the invisible God, the firstborn of all creation. For by him all things were created, in heaven and on earth, visible and invisible, whether thrones or dominions or rulers or authorities—all things were created through him and for him. And he is before all things, and in him all things hold together. . . . For in him all the fullness of God was pleased to dwell, and through him to reconcile to himself all things, whether on earth or in heaven, making peace by the blood of his cross. (Colossians 1:15–17, 19–20)*

Again, we must understand why God made everything and why this age is what it is to fully participate in God's plan. This understanding is so critical that Paul emphasized it throughout his letters.[1] Paul summarized his grasp of reality most concisely in Romans 1:

---

[1] For example, 1 Corinthians 1:18–2:5; Ephesians 1:3–23.

> *For his invisible attributes, namely, his eternal power and divine nature, have been clearly perceived, ever since the creation of the world, in the things that have been made. (v. 20)*

God has made His invisible attributes *known* through creation. This is the first part of God's purpose for the created realm. Creation not only shows God's power, it is a stage to reveal God's *nature*. God's attributes were invisible and unknown, so He formed this cosmos as an immersive classroom so we could discover Him. This implies that God cannot be fully known apart from His creation. This has been true since the beginning but was fully revealed when God became part of His creation in Jesus.

This has a profound implication: If you do not prioritize seeking out the revelation of God in this age, you do not understand why you have been created or the purpose for your life. God's revelation of Himself drove Him to create, but that revelation is inseparable from the second part of God's purpose for this age: *God is forming a people to become His eternal companion.*

THE UNFOLDING PLAN

From the very beginning, God created man to be His image.[2] This does not simply indicate man was made like God; it reveals God decided to make His image known to the created realm in a human form. When God made all things, He set into motion a plan to reveal Himself in a divine human *and* in a people. Jesus is God's image, but we are God's image as well. Jesus and His people both make God known. W. Ross Blackburn explains:

> Because humanity is the image of God the command calls for God's image to spread throughout, and ultimately fill, the earth. Furthermore, as humanity spreads throughout the earth, he is called to exercise dominion, governing God's creation as befits his status as God's image. The effect of the commandment, then, is that life on the earth would witness to

---

[2]Genesis 1:26; 5:1; 9:6; 1 Corinthians 11:7; 15:47–49; Colossians 3:10; James 3:9.

the character of God, as God's image spreads and governs according to his likeness and character.[3]

God did not abandon His plan in the fall. For example, when God delivered Israel from Egypt, His primary goal was to reveal Himself,[4] and He chose to do it in a very specific way:

> Throughout Exodus, the Lord is known as the God of a particular people, and is not known apart from them.[5]

When we grasp God's plan, we see that Adam and Eve were the first missionaries because they were given the task of spreading the knowledge of God through creation by living as His image so He could be made known. In the same way, Israel was formed as a missionary nation in the exodus:

> . . . it is through a people formed as a "holy nation" (Exod. 19:6; 1 Pet. 2:9) that the Lord realizes his missionary purposes throughout the world.[6]

God formed Israel to make Himself known to the world. Israel was (and remains) part of God's missionary purpose. Incidentally, this is why God has not abandoned Israel. On Mount Sinai, God "married" Israel.[7] Using Paul's analogy, God as the "head" of Israel joined Himself to Israel as His "body." God brought forth His Son through Israel, but if God joined Himself to Israel in this way, then God must also form Israel into His image so that He might be made known. There is something about God that must be made known through Israel, and He is not finished with the people He first chose.

---

[3] W. Ross Blackburn, *The God Who Makes Himself Known: The Missionary Heart of the Book of Exodus*, ed. D. A. Carson, vol. 28, New Studies in Biblical Theology (England; Downers Grove, IL: Apollos; InterVarsity Press, 2012), 29.

[4] W. Ross Blackburn, *The God Who Makes Himself Known*, 40.

[5] W. Ross Blackburn, *The God Who Makes Himself Known*, 57.

[6] W. Ross Blackburn, *The God Who Makes Himself Known*, 79.

[7] Isaiah 54:5; Jeremiah 2:2; 3:14; 31:32; Hosea 2:7.

Some people ask, "Why doesn't God just appear in some dramatic way if He wants people to know Him?" The Bible has a clear answer to this: God wants to be known, and He has always sought to make Himself known through a people. This was His plan in the garden, it was His plan in the days of the Old Testament, and it remains His plan. The New Testament is church-centric because the apostles understood God would reveal Himself through His people.

If you want to engage in missions, and you should, building the church is the most missionary thing you can do because God wants to put Himself on display through a people.

Mass evangelism is not enough to fulfill the task of missions, nor should we expect God to take a new approach. God wants to be known through His image. Even when God returns to the earth, He will return as a man and dwell on the earth as God in human form.[8]

Do you realize you were made to reveal God to the created realm?

This is your calling, and it should define your life because God wants to make Himself known through you. You cannot image God without the Spirit of God. God will transform us into His image, but we must respond and allow Him to transform us. And then we must disciple others so they may be transformed.

HE IS THE HEAD OF A BODY

Paul's summary of God's will in Colossians is very concise, so it is easy to miss all that he says. After presenting creation and this age as God's stage, Paul gives the second part of God's purpose for this age:

> *And he is the head of the body, the church. He is the beginning, the firstborn from the dead, that in everything he might be preeminent. (Colossians 1:18)*

This verse must be read in light of Colossians 1:15–17, where Paul defined God's will as God's desire to reveal Himself through creation in the person of Jesus. Colossians 1:18–20 adds an astonishing detail to God's plan: Jesus is the Head of a corporate body made up of redeemed people, and this identity establishes His prominence over

---

[8]Psalm 45; 47:2–7; 98; 99; 118; Isaiah 2:2–4; 49:7; Jeremiah 10:10; Ezekiel 20:33; Micah 4:1–3; Zechariah 8:3; 8:20–23; 14:9, 17; Revelation 11:15; 19:11–16.

every other thing. Let this sink in: The revelation of Jesus' glory is inseparably tied to His people.

God created everything in creation to make Himself known, but He has formed the church for a unique function. The revelation of Jesus in the context of the church reveals Jesus' matchless superiority.

There is a revelation of God that must come through the church. It is the highest revelation of God in the created realm, and this revelation reveals His preeminence over everything that has been made. If we do not grasp the connection between the revelation of God and a people, we do not know the will of God and cannot be "fully pleasing" to Him.[9]

Paul described Jesus as the "beginning," and this description has a double meaning. First, it reminded the Colossians of Paul's previous point that Jesus is the origin for all creation. He is the *beginning* of all creation—the One for whom everything was made. Ancient readers would have connected this description of Jesus to the opening words of the Bible, "In the beginning. . . ."[10] Paul wanted to make sure we understood Jesus was at the beginning of the entire creation story.

Paul also had a second meaning in mind for "beginning." This time he connected it to Jesus as the first resurrected Human. Jesus was the *beginning* of all creation and the *beginning* of a resurrected humanity. Jesus inseparably joined Himself to the cosmos by becoming a part of creation,[11] and He is inseparably joined to His people. A head cannot exist apart from a body; therefore, Jesus as the Head must be connected to His body.

All of creation is a stage to reveal God's person, and the new humanity is also a "stage" to reveal God.

Humanity is a stage in the sense that God chose to fully reveal Himself in a man, but there is more to it. God is going to reveal Himself in one Man (Jesus) *and* in a people joined to that Man. Both revelations are required for God to be made known in the way He wants to be known.

---

[9]Colossians 1:10.

[10]Genesis 1:1.

[11]John 1:14; Romans 8:3; Galatians 4:4.

39 WHAT DOES GOD WANT?

Jesus is the beginning of all creation and the beginning (Head and firstborn) of a new humanity. Yet, Jesus is incomplete without His people. His people will demonstrate His prominence in all things which implies Jesus' prominence is not fully known apart from His people. Jesus is preeminent because He reveals the nature of God in the cosmos *and* in the new humanity. Both are required to fully reveal His majesty.

The head is the highest, most prominent part of a person. It is where a person's nature, intelligence, emotions, and identity are found. The head leads the body, and the body cannot function without the head. If you only see a person's head, however, you do not really see the person because the head is only a small part of a person.[12] Furthermore, a head not attached to a body is appalling.

The implications are astounding: The revelation of Jesus is incomplete without His people. Jesus apart from His people is like seeing a person's head without a body.

Jesus was the beginning of all creation. When He finished what we read in Genesis 1, He set into motion a process that produced a stage for His revelation in His incarnation, suffering, death, resurrection, and ascension. His first coming opened up the mystery set into motion when He began the cosmos. Jesus is also the beginning of the church, and the pattern is the same. Jesus began a process that is going to become a stage for the revelation of His nature through a corporate people. They will become a stage, and His glory will be made known.

No one expected the revelation of God that came when Jesus became a man. Neither is anyone fully expecting the revelation of God that is going to come through His people. Jesus set something into motion that has not yet been fully revealed.

The revelation of Jesus that must come through His people is one of the most important but often overlooked end-time themes.

Paul wanted the Colossians to know that the revelation of Jesus in creation is incomplete until Jesus is made known in a body. The Head of the body is now visible, but without the body it is an incomplete revelation. God's plan to fully reveal Himself in creation is incomplete

---

[12]Approximately 10 percent of the surface area of the body, see https://en.wikipedia.org/wiki/Total_body_surface_area/.

until He reveals His Son in a people. There are aspects of His person He will not reveal any other way.

All of this is part of God's will. He is not engaged in His creation out of obligation, and the plan of redemption is not simply a rescue scheme. God has designed everything in this fallen age—even His intense suffering—for His own pleasure:

> *For in him all the fullness of God was pleased to dwell, and through him to reconcile to himself all things, whether on earth or in heaven, making peace by the blood of his cross. (Colossians 1:19–20)*

God experienced intense delight when He joined Himself to creation. He did not become a man and suffer intensely to rescue a cosmos that had gone off track. He became a man and suffered because He took incredible pleasure in being made known. He *wanted* us to know who He was, and He has enjoyed every aspect of it. He planned it all from the very beginning for the sake of joy.[13]

God's burning desire to make Himself known gave birth to the cosmos, and it gave birth to a new humanity. He is the Head of this new humanity, and He will finish what He started.

THE FULL REVELATION OF GOD
Just as there are aspects of God that cannot be known apart from His incarnation in the person of Jesus, there are aspects of who God is that cannot be known apart from who He is in His people.

When we see Jesus but not His people, it is an incomplete revelation of who God is.[14] Paul grasped that the glory of Jesus must be revealed in a people, but have we? Are we content with the revelation of a Jesus who dwells in the heavens, whom we hope to see when we die, or do we have a vision for the revelation of Jesus *now*, in this age, in a people who are formed like Him?

Are we content with a limited revelation of who God is? If we love Him and long for Him and desire Him, we must be eager to know

---

[13] Isaiah 62:4–5; 65:19; Jeremiah 32:41; Zephaniah 3:17; John 15:11; Hebrews 1:9.

[14] Jesus is *fully* God in every way. He makes God known, and while He is not incomplete, the revelation God wants to give through Him is incomplete without a people who are transformed into the Son's image.

Jesus in the way He has chosen to reveal Himself, and this means we must pursue the revelation of Jesus in a people.

God will reveal the majesty of His Son in an unprecedented way in His return, but before that return He will reveal the glory of His Son in a people who come to maturity and become like Him.[15] This people will become so much like Jesus that the way they live in the end-time crisis will demonstrate the life of Jesus. The Father revealed Himself in an unprecedented way in the life, suffering, and exaltation of Jesus in the first century, and He is going to do something similar through a people at the end of the age.

God will be revealed to us in an unprecedented way in the end-time life, suffering, and exaltation of a people.

Just as we saw God in ways we had never seen Him in the person of Jesus, so also we will see God in ways we have never seen Him in the mature end-time church. God is going to continue His revelation of Himself in Jesus by producing a *body* who will resemble the *Head*.

Do we have a vision for the revelation of God in a people that is as shocking and surprising as God's own incarnation in Jesus? Nothing can match the revelation of God in Jesus, but we must not minimize the majesty of the revelation of God in a people. This has not come to fullness yet, but it will.

Nearly two thousand years ago Paul described the church as the "fullness" of God:

> *And he put all things under his feet and gave him as head over all things to the church, which is his body, the fullness of him who fills all in all. (Ephesians 1:22–23)*

The church has been the "fullness" of Jesus for nearly two thousand years, yet even we believers do not grasp our true identity. However, the age will not end until God reveals the true nature of His people and what Jesus accomplished in His suffering. If we want to fully partner with God, we must see the church and relate to other believers as the fullness of Jesus. This understanding of our true reality must permeate our approach to discipleship.

---

[15] Romans 8:29; 1 Corinthians 15:49; 2 Corinthians 3:18; 4:10–11; 1 John 3:2.

When we ask God to reveal the beauty of His Son, do we grasp that we are asking Him, in part, to reveal Himself in and through a people?

This "new humanity" is the "new creation" that Paul speaks about in other places. It is so different from the way we are born that Paul says it is "not Greek and Jew, circumcised and uncircumcised, barbarian, Scythian, slave, or free."[16] This is an entirely new kind of humanity. It has been transformed by the revelation of Jesus to reveal Jesus and make Him known. This is the new creation. This is the church. This is what God wants.

The body of Jesus is His Bride,[17] and when we reflect on this, we typically emphasize God's extravagant affections for His people and His desire for intimacy with them. The church exists entirely because of God's desire, so this is the right starting point, but it is not the entire truth of what it means for the church to be a "bride."

If we are Jesus' Bride, it means we are part of His story and take part in His calling. It means we have intense affection for Him and surrender our destiny and our identity to find a new identity in Him. This is what it means to be the Bride of Christ. Somehow, we have made it all about us when it really is all about Him.

When we speak about the church, do we speak with this in mind? When we pray for the church, do we pray with this in mind? When we are frustrated or disappointed by what we see in the church, do we have more confidence in what we can see or in what God has said about His people?

We need more confidence in what the Bible says about the church and her future than what we can observe with our own eyes.

Discipleship is the way we partner with God to produce this people. Is your plan for discipleship designed to produce this?

A NEW ADAM AND A NEW PEOPLE
The mystery of Jesus is connected to God's ability to form a new people.

Now that God has revealed the mystery of His plan, we can look back on redemptive history and see this was always His intention. In the book of Genesis, God's answer to man's rebellion was to predict

---

[16]Colossians 3:11.

[17]Ephesians 5:22–32; Revelation 19:7–9.

salvation would come through the "seed" of a woman.[18] This mysterious prediction pointed to a new man who would be joined to humanity. If a new man was the answer to the fall, then it is reasonable that God would form a new humanity. Furthermore, God appeared to the prophets in physical form, repeatedly hinting that the new man would also be divine.[19]

There is a strong symmetry between the opening of Genesis and our present age. There was darkness and chaos. There were waters that needed to be divided and shaped. Beasts were created, and then man was formed to rule the beasts.[20] God first made Adam. He was not deficient in any way, but he was incomplete. God's creation was not complete until He created a companion for Adam. This companion was fully compatible with Adam, made from him, and yet distinct from him. Humanity was not complete until she was made.

In many ways, this is a picture of this age. We experience darkness and chaos. The nations are often allegorized in Scripture as the waters or storm seas. The spiritual powers who rule in this age are often symbolized as "beasts." However, in the midst of this present chaos, God is bringing forth a people. They are a new creation, and they are His prize creation. They will subdue and rule the "beasts" of this age.[21] When you read the Bible carefully, you discover, as we have seen, that Adam was just a beginning. God's purpose all along was a *new* humanity taken from Adam but remade—a humanity made not just in Adam's image, but in Jesus' image.[22] Jesus is God's final Adam, and God's work of redemption through Him is not complete until this "Adam" has a compatible companion.

If Jesus is superior to Adam, and we are transformed into Jesus' image, it means we will resemble Jesus much more than we now resemble Adam.

---

[18] Genesis 3:15.

[19] Genesis 16:7–11; 21:17; 22:11–16; 31:11; 32:24–30; Exodus 3:2; 23:21–24; Numbers 20:16; 22:22–35; Judges 2:1–4; 6:11–22; 13:3–21; Isaiah 6:1; Ezekiel 1:26; Daniel 7:13; Zechariah 1:11; 3:1–6.

[20] Genesis 1.

[21] Daniel 7:27; Luke 10:19; 1 Corinthians 6:3; Romans 16:20.

[22] Romans 8:29; 1 Corinthians 15:49; 2 Corinthians 3:18; 4:10–11; 1 John 3:2.

Filling Up What Is Lacking in Jesus' Afflictions

Near the end of Colossians 1, Paul wrote an astounding statement:

> *Now I rejoice in my sufferings for your sake, and in my flesh I am filling up what is lacking in Christ's afflictions for the sake of his body, that is, the church. (v. 24)*

At first glance this is a shocking statement—what could possibly be "lacking" in Jesus' suffering? Obviously, Jesus' suffering perfectly secured God's mercy, so Paul must have something else in mind. If we read this in context to the entire chapter, it becomes much clearer.[23]

As we have seen, the main theme of the chapter is God's desire to fully reveal Himself in creation through His Son and His people. God wants a flesh-and-blood revelation of Himself. God is revealed most deeply in His suffering, but very few actually saw His suffering. Furthermore, Jesus has ascended into the heavens and is not currently visible in the flesh. The thing that is "lacking" is that the vast majority of people do not have the chance to see God in the flesh revealing Himself in His life and especially in His suffering. God has a spectacular answer to this "lack": *He is maturing a corporate people who will be a flesh-and-blood revelation of Jesus.*

John Piper explains:

> God intends for the afflictions of Christ to be presented to the world through the afflictions of his people. God really means for the body of Christ, the church, to experience some of the suffering he experienced so that when we offer the Christ of the cross to people, they see the Christ of the cross in us. We are to make the afflictions of Christ real for people by the afflictions we experience in offering him to them, and living the life of love he lived. . . . The suffering love of Christ for sinners is seen in the suffering love of his people for sinners.[24]

---

[23] John Piper, "Filling Up What Is Lacking in Christ's Afflictions," https://www.desiringgod.org/messages/filling-up-what-is-lacking-in-christs-afflictions/, accessed November 5, 2020.

[24] John Piper, "To Finish the Aim of Christ's Afflictions," https://www.desiringgod.org/messages/to-finish-the-aim-of-christs-afflictions/, accessed November 13, 2020.

Paul rejoiced in his sufferings because they created a context where Jesus could be revealed in the flesh and the churches he served could encounter a revelation of God they could not otherwise see. Paul in his flesh became a demonstration of Jesus in the flesh for the sake of the church. The knowledge of God was made known to the church through Paul *in Paul's flesh*.

Paul became a revelation of the incarnation, not in a way that deified him, but in a way that profoundly made Christ known and compelled the church also to become a demonstration of Christ. Because God has been revealed most completely in His suffering, what the church experienced through Paul was transformational. It made up the *lack* that came from not being present in Jesus' suffering.

There is something very deep about God revealed in His afflictions, and He wants that made known to all people and all creation. In this sense, Paul was a prototype. This age will end with a brief moment of intense suffering.[25] In that suffering, God will reveal Himself through His body in a way we cannot now anticipate. God will be made known again in suffering through a corporate people who display the nature of God. This will reveal Jesus in an undeniable way, and as we will see shortly, Jesus asked the Father to bring it about.

Before Jesus returns, the world will encounter Him through His people—are you willing to share the apostle's joy in revealing God in your own flesh?

---

[25] Jeremiah 30:7; Daniel 12:1; Matthew 24:21; Revelation 12:11.

HE MUST BE REVEALED

The first coming of Jesus was an unprecedented and unparalleled revelation of God. It opened up the "mystery" of who God is.[1] While God's incarnation, His suffering, and all that surrounded these are probably the ultimate revelation of who God is—certainly the ultimate revelation of God in this age—it is not the end of God's plan to reveal Himself. The events of the end of this age that accompany the return of Jesus are also known as the "revelation" of Jesus:

> *The revelation of Jesus Christ, which God gave him to show to his servants the things that must soon take place. He made it known by sending his angel to his servant John. (Revelation 1:1)*

The word *revelation* is *apokalypsis* (ἀποκάλυψις), which is commonly translated into English as *apocalypse*. The word literally means "unveiling." While many people assume an apocalypse is a great disaster, the original word describes the revelation of a person or a thing. Accordingly, the events that surround the end of the age are an *unveiling* of Jesus, and this shows God has much more to reveal about His Son.

When we think about the end of this age, we often focus on the end-time trouble, God's judgments, or the man known as "the beast" (the antichrist), but that is only one aspect of the end of the age. Dramatic and unprecedented events will surround the return of Jesus, but those events have a specific purpose. They set the stage for the *unveiling* of Jesus.

---

[1] Matthew 13:11; Mark 4:11; Luke 8:10; Romans 16:25; 1 Corinthians 2:7; 4:1; Ephesians 1:9; 3:3–4, 9; 5:32; 6:19; Colossians 1:26–27; 2:2; 4:3; 1 Timothy 3:16.

Revelation 1:1 is not the only description of the end of the age as an unveiling of Jesus. The apostles frequently described the end of the age in this way:

> *So that you are not lacking in any gift, as you wait for the revealing of our Lord Jesus Christ. (1 Corinthians 1:7)*

> *And to grant relief to you who are afflicted as well as to us, when the Lord Jesus is revealed from heaven with his mighty angels. (2 Thessalonians 1:7)*

> *So that the tested genuineness of your faith—more precious than gold that perishes though it is tested by fire—may be found to result in praise and glory and honor at the revelation of Jesus Christ. (1 Peter 1:7)*

> *Therefore, preparing your minds for action, and being sober-minded, set your hope fully on the grace that will be brought to you at the revelation of Jesus Christ. (v. 13)*

> *But rejoice insofar as you share Christ's sufferings, that you may also rejoice and be glad when his glory is revealed. (4:13)*

In each of these verses, the end of the age is described as an apocalypse or revelation of Jesus because *all things* exist to reveal God, and this includes the events of the end of the age.[2] This includes the person we typically refer to as the *antichrist*. Even he will ultimately serve God's purposes of making Jesus known.

THE APOCALYPSE OF THE CHURCH

If Jesus will be revealed (unveiled) at the end of the age, and His glory and preeminence are connected to His people, then it follows that Jesus will be revealed and glorified in His people at the end of the age. This unveiling will begin before Jesus returns and climax at His return in a way that will shock and amaze us all.

The apostles not only expected the revelation of Jesus, they also understood the revelation of Jesus *in a people* was directly connected to the end of the age:

---

[2] Revelation 19:10.

> *For I consider that the sufferings of this present time are not worth comparing with the glory that is to be revealed to us. For the creation waits with eager longing for the revealing of the sons of God. (Romans 8:18–19)*

All of creation is longing for the unveiling (apocalypse) of the sons of God.[3]

Paul described the end-time unveiling of the people of God as an apocalypse because God's end-time revelation of Jesus is connected to the unveiling of a stunning people who are like Him. The *Head* must have a *body*. This age is God's stage to glorify the Head, and it is also His stage to produce a glorified body. The age will not end until God produces this people, so creation is *longing* for the apocalypse of God's people.

Paul goes on in Romans 8 to say creation *and* the Holy Spirit are *groaning* for the revelation of God's people.[4] And Paul expects the church to be groaning,[5] which leads us to a critical question: *Are we groaning for the revelation of God's people?* Do we share Paul's insight into the "apocalypse" of God's people? Do we realize who the redeemed really are even though we currently dwell in weak and fallen bodies? Do we invest in each other and the church with this in mind?

When Jesus comes, He will be glorified *in His people* who will also marvel at His majesty:

> *When he comes on that day to be glorified in his saints, and to be marveled at among all who have believed. . . . (2 Thessalonians 1:10)*

Second Thessalonians captures the two aspects of the end-time apocalypse. The people of God will be unveiled in glory, and then Jesus will be unveiled in glory. Jesus' glory is clearly superior because the saints will marvel at His glory and not their own, but we cannot minimize what God wants to reveal in His people. This is not a

---

[3] In context, "sons" means both male and female children.

[4] Romans 8:22, 26.

[5] Romans 8:23.

peripheral idea; the apostles repeatedly predicted God was going to glorify Himself in a people at the end of the age:[6]

> *But our citizenship is in heaven, and from it we await a Savior, the Lord Jesus Christ, who will transform our lowly body to be like his glorious body, by the power that enables him even to subject all things to himself. (Philippians 3:20–21)*

> *We exhorted each one of you and encouraged you and charged you to walk in a manner worthy of God, who calls you into his own kingdom and glory. (1 Thessalonians 2:12)*

> *To this he called you through our gospel, so that you may obtain the glory of our Lord Jesus Christ. (2 Thessalonians 2:14)*

> *Beloved, we are God's children now, and what we will be has not yet appeared; but we know that when he appears we shall be like him, because we shall see him as he is. (1 John 3:2)*

These statements are astounding:

- God will transform our bodies to become like His.
- Jesus calls us to participate in His kingdom (rule) and His glory.
- The gospel is a message that calls us to share Jesus' own glory.
- We will be like Jesus in appearance.

Each of these predictions reveals God's goal for discipleship. Discipleship is the process that beholds the glory of God in the person of Jesus and then works with God to see a people become like Him, being transformed into His image.[7]

Christians speak often about the beauty of Jesus, but God wants that beauty to be embodied in a people. Consequently, we cannot be content with only speaking about Jesus' beauty. Obviously, His people

---

[6] This idea was not new to the New Testament. For example, Daniel 7:27; 11:33–35; 12:3.

[7] For more on this, see the companion book *Discipleship Begins With Beholding*.

cannot display the fullness of His beauty, but they must become an authentic witness of it.

THE HOPE OF THE GOSPEL

Paul finished Colossians 1 by reminding the Colossians that their and our future glory is the hope of the gospel:

> *And you, who once were alienated and hostile in mind, doing evil deeds, he has now reconciled in his body of flesh by his death, in order to present you holy and blameless and above reproach before him, if indeed you continue in the faith, stable and steadfast, not shifting from the hope of the gospel that you heard, which has been proclaimed in all creation under heaven, and of which I, Paul, became a minister. (vv. 21–23)*

When we read these verses in light of everything we have already seen, they become even more glorious. When we were hostile to God, Jesus paid a terrible price in His own body so He could present us holy and blameless. Jesus did not die only so we could be forgiven; He purchased our forgiveness so that a people could be presented to Him in splendor. This is the "hope of the gospel" that the apostles proclaimed.

The hope of the gospel is not forgiveness and a heavenly retirement. The hope of the gospel is the hope of being part of the majestic, corporate people God will present to His Son as the reward for His suffering.

Discipleship is designed to prepare individuals to participate in the great apocalypse of the people who belong to Jesus. Whatever you do in life, spend your life so you will be part of this people *and* so that others can also become a part of this people.

THE HOPE OF GLORY

Colossians 1 concludes with a summary of Paul's assignment among the churches:

> *I became a minister according to the stewardship from God that was given to me for you, to make the word of God fully known, the mystery hidden for ages and generations but now revealed to his saints. To them God chose to make known how great among the Gentiles are the riches of the glory of this mystery, which is Christ in you, the hope of glory. Him we proclaim, warning everyone and teaching everyone with all wisdom, that*

> *we may present everyone mature in Christ. For this I toil, struggling with all his energy that he powerfully works within me. (vv. 25–29)*

The main points of Paul's assignment can be summarized as follows:

- Paul was given a divine stewardship to make God's intentions fully known.
- God's purposes have been a mystery hidden for the ages, but it has now been revealed.
- The glory of this mystery is Jesus in His people.
- The presence of Jesus in His people produces the "hope of glory." The word *hope* (ἐλπίς) carries the idea of confidence in something good that has not yet come.[8] There is a glory coming that is not yet seen.
- Paul and his team proclaim Jesus, warning and teaching everyone with wisdom. This wisdom is the wisdom of living in light of God's purposes.
- Paul and his team labor to present the church mature in Jesus. Contextually, this means presenting the church mature when Jesus returns.[9]
- Paul's work was hard work and a constant struggle. It was not simple or easy. However, he was empowered by God's Spirit that powerfully worked within him.

A mystery has been revealed: God is going to share Himself with His people and put His glory in them. This revelation drove Paul and his team to tirelessly teach, encourage, and warn people to live lives of wisdom in light of the glory God has prepared for them. Paul's plan of discipleship had a specific goal in mind: to see the church presented to Jesus at His return as a mature people. He understood God's purpose to mature a church at the end of the age.

---

[8] Johannes P. Louw and Eugene Albert Nida, *Greek-English Lexicon of the New Testament: Based on Semantic Domains* (New York: United Bible Societies, 1996), 295.

[9] F. F. Bruce, *The Epistles to the Colossians, to Philemon, and to the Ephesians*, The New International Commentary on the New Testament (Grand Rapids, MI: Wm. B. Eerdmans Publishing Co., 1984), 87.

Discipleship is messy, and Paul had to deal with an incredible number of issues in the church. He struggled constantly and was often exhausted, but he was not discouraged. God's power worked powerfully within him because this was God's plan and God's desire—God is the One who wants a people like Him clothed in His own glory.

Paul's confidence in God's plan to mature a people gave him strength to continue to disciple people despite their betrayals, accusations, sins, shortcomings, and all manner of constant challenges.

Colossians 1 was not the only time Paul described his desire to present a people mature to Jesus at His coming. In Ephesians, Paul revealed the ministry gifts given in the church have been given until the church comes to fully maturity, which will be measured by the status of the fullness of Jesus:

> *And he gave the apostles, the prophets, the evangelists, the shepherds and teachers, to equip the saints for the work of ministry, for building up the body of Christ, until we all attain to the unity of the faith and of the knowledge of the Son of God, to mature manhood, to the measure of the stature of the fullness of Christ. (Ephesians 4:11–13)*

Paul was laboring with confidence that God was going to mature a corporate people and make them just like Jesus. He understood this people will come to maturity and be clothed with glory at the end of the age. Our labor is God's own labor because He is working to present a glorious church to Himself:

> *Christ loved the church and gave himself up for her, that he might sanctify her, having cleansed her by the washing of water with the word, so that he might present the church to himself in splendor, without spot or wrinkle or any such thing, that she might be holy and without blemish. (Ephesians 5:25–27)*

Paul's conviction in God's plan to bring a people to maturity drove his discipleship, and it should drive ours as well. Paul frequently described his pastoral ministry using the analogy of presenting a bride to a husband:

> *For I feel a divine jealousy for you, since I betrothed you to one husband, to present you as a pure virgin to Christ. (2 Corinthians 11:2)*

This analogy reveals quite a bit about how the apostles viewed God's plan for the church in this age.

A COMPATIBLE COMPANION

Revelation 19 describes the end of the age and the incredible moment Paul labored for:

> *After this I heard what seemed to be the loud voice of a great multitude in heaven, crying out, "Hallelujah! Salvation and glory and power belong to our God." (v. 1)*

> *Let us rejoice and exult and give him the glory, for the marriage of the Lamb has come, and his Bride has made herself ready; it was granted her to clothe herself with fine linen, bright and pure"—for the fine linen is the righteous deeds of the saints. And the angel said to me, "Write this: Blessed are those who are invited to the marriage supper of the Lamb." And he said to me, "These are the true words of God." (vv. 7–9)*

As we have seen, this age exists to produce a companion for God, and when He has His companion, the age will end.

God's people will make themselves ready (v. 7), implying active partnership with God. We must cooperate with Him, respond to Him, and allow Him to shape us into His image. The Bride will not become ready passively. Her readiness will require real desire and real effort. Once the corporate people of God are ready to be joined to Him and clothed in His glory, the age will end.

Longing for Jesus' return is not about getting your timeline exactly right (though we should know what the Bible says about times and seasons). Longing for His return is living a life of desire—a life where, like a bride, you long to become His companion and live with intentionality as you prepare for that day.

If the Bride does not desire the day of His appearing, she will not take the steps necessary (discipleship) to prepare for Him. When we do not wholeheartedly engage in discipleship, it reveals our lack of interest in Jesus' day and His reward.

Throughout the Bible, marriage is used as an analogy for God's relationship with His people and especially for Jesus' relationship with the redeemed.[10] Using this analogy has a profound implication: *Two*

---

[10]Isaiah 54:5–7; Jeremiah 2:2; 31:32; Ezekiel 16:8; Hosea 2:2; Romans 8:29; 1 Corinthians 15:49; 2 Corinthians 3:18; 4:10–11; 1 John 3:2.

individuals must be compatible to be married. Marriage is not a relationship between two *identical* persons, but it is a relationship between two *compatible* persons. When John heard heaven declare the "Bride has made herself ready" and "the marriage supper of the Lamb has come," heaven was proclaiming the church will become *compatible* to be joined to God so deeply that marriage is the closest human analogy for the way Jesus will be joined to His people.

The idea of humans becoming this compatible to God should make the angels cry out, *"This is unjust! How can God possibly join Himself to those who rebelled against Him? Furthermore, these humans are merely creatures!"* However, we do not read a single statement to this effect. When the Bride comes to maturity, the angels do not declare an injustice as we would expect; instead, they cry out, "Let us rejoice, and be glad, and give Him the glory." They are stunned by God's ability to take people who rebelled against Him and transform these people into His image so completely that the people are now compatible with Him.

Once God gets what He wants—a corporate people drawn from all people who come to maturity—this age will end.

Revelation 19 describes Jesus as the Bridegroom of a majestic bride, and Colossians 1 refers to Him as the "Head" of a body. Just as the Head must have His body, the Bridegroom must have His Bride. If Jesus is a bridegroom, God must present Him with a bride who is compatible to Him.

We cannot fully anticipate how glorious Jesus' reward in His people is going to be. Jesus did not die to receive half-hearted affection from a compromised bride. The end-time church is going to be more spectacular than we can imagine. In the same way, a head without a body is not glorious but odd, God's plan to exalt His Son must be finished by producing a body that is appropriate for the Head.

Jesus suffered tremendously and has been waiting for two thousand years for the fullness of His reward in a people. Imagine what the Father feels about His Son and what He has prepared for Him. The Father is going to give His Son the most spectacular Bride anyone can imagine as a just reward for His suffering.

Jesus is not fully revealed or glorified until the Father produces a bride who is a compatible companion and a body that is suitable to Him as the Head.

THE END-TIME REVELATION OF THE CHURCH

Nothing can or will ever compare to the revelation of God in Jesus, but God has a second act in mind. God shocked everyone by revealing Himself in a human body, and He is going to shock the world by revealing Himself again in His corporate body, the mature church. The world is not expecting this. Tragically, most of the church does not expect it either. Few have studied it, we rarely speak about it, and there is little vision for it. Paul understood and expected this. He labored for it and gave his life for it. He longed for it.[11] Do we?

Paul prayed continuously that the Colossians would understand this because, if you do not understand God's purpose for this age, you cannot live in a way that is fully pleasing to Him. This wisdom provoked Paul to patient endurance and committed discipleship. Does our grasp of the end times do the same? If not, we have not understood the end-time message correctly.

---

[11] 1 Corinthians 4:14; 2 Corinthians 11:2; Galatians 4:11, 17–19; Philippians 1:8; Colossians 1:28–29; 1 Thessalonians 2:10–12.

A Life of Wisdom

A life of wisdom is a life aligned with God's desire (will) for this age:

- God's revelation of Himself in the person of Jesus, particularly in His suffering.
- God's formation of a people who are shaped by the context of this age to become like Him.

If you want to be a disciple, everything in your life should be aligned with these two purposes, and if you align your life with these two purposes, you will be successful.

If you discover who God is and allow Him to make you like Him, even great failures or losses in your life can become redemptive. It is important to be faithful in the assignments the Lord gives us, but those assignments do not always end in "success" the way we typically define success. Ideas do not always succeed. Organizations come to an end. Outcomes that that we hoped for may not come to pass. We sometimes make serious mistakes that have long-term repercussions because of our ignorance or weakness.

If you focus your life on the pursuit of the knowledge of God and allow Him to shape you in His image, you will be massively successful.

Your business may or may not make it. Your "ministry" may or may not seem big. Your life may not feel "successful." You may face unexpected challenges or be given unexpected opportunities. Your assignment may end up "bigger" than you imagined or much "smaller" than you were hoping. In the end, it does not matter as long as you align your life with God's will—His two purposes for the age.

Even profound failures can move you forward if you cooperate with God's will. For example, Peter was called to pastor, but he was strong, brash, and arrogant. Then, when Jesus was betrayed, Peter publicly and completely denied Jesus. Jesus' response was incredible. He sought Peter out. He sat with Peter and asked Peter three times if Peter truly loved Him. Peter had denied Jesus three times, so each question addressed one of the denials. Jesus followed Peter's affirmations of love with an instruction: "Feed my sheep."[1]

Most of us would expect Peter's denial to disqualify him for future ministry, but Jesus used this failure to prepare Peter for his assignment. Peter would no longer be an arrogant and brash pastor. He could now become a tender, humbled pastor. Going forward, he would be patient with others when they failed and came up short. Peter's greatest failure moved him forward because he responded to the Lord.

Faithfulness is important in an assignment, but the outcome of the assignment depends on the Lord. So many need to be free from the pressure to be "successful" according to the definition of this age. If you read the Bible, many (perhaps most) of the great figures were not successful according to this world's definition of success. Jesus warned us that we do not always evaluate success correctly. Many who think they are successful now really aren't, and many who think they are not great actually are.[2] We are going to be shocked in the age to come, so we must live with wisdom now by orienting our lives around God's two-fold purpose for this age.

Once you grasp that this age is only really about two purposes, you can easily align yourself with God's purposes and walk in agreement with Him.

You can live according to this two-fold purpose whether the scope of your life is large or small. You can do it whether you are in "ministry" or not. You can do it if your business succeeds or fails. Jesus lived the vast majority of His life in obscurity in a small village doing manual labor to show what a successful life can look like.

If you grow in the knowledge of God and allow God to make you like Him, you will win, and you will hear "well done" when you see the Lord face to face.

We were made to discover God and become like Him. The enemy knows how intoxicating God truly is, so he rages against the revelation of God with every scheme possible. He does not want us to catch a

---

[1] John 21:15–17.

[2] Matthew 19:30; Mark 10:31; Luke 13:30.

glimpse of God's divine beauty and the future God has for His people because it exposes the ugly nature of everything he uses to seduce us.

The enemy will do everything he can to distract you from these two purposes in life. He will even use success in ministry or business to divert your attention. He will give you any number of alternate ways to measure success and impact. However, in the end it is only these two things that ultimately matter in this age.

We all long to be known and to search out mysteries. The most profound mystery to be explored is God, and that mystery can dwell within us by the Holy Spirit.

Does your pursuit of God correspond to His zeal and desire to be known?

THE HEAVENLY MAN

Paul summarized his gospel in 1 Corinthians 15 and concluded it with a description of Jesus as the Exalted Man in the heavens:[3]

> *There is one glory of the sun, and another glory of the moon, and another glory of the stars; for star differs from star in glory. So is it with the resurrection of the dead. What is sown is perishable; what is raised is imperishable. It is sown in dishonor; it is raised in glory. It is sown in weakness; it is raised in power. It is sown a natural body; it is raised a spiritual body. If there is a natural body, there is also a spiritual body. Thus it is written, "The first man Adam became a living being"; the last Adam became a life-giving spirit. . . . The first man was from the earth, a man of dust; the second man is from heaven. As was the man of dust, so also are those who are of the dust, and as is the man of heaven, so also are those who are of heaven. Just as we have borne the image of the man of dust, we shall also bear the image of the man of heaven. . . . Behold! I tell you a mystery. We shall not all sleep, but we shall all be changed. . . . For this perishable body must put on the imperishable, and this mortal body must put on immortality. (vv. 41–45, 47–49, 51–53)*

Paul's idea of a "heavenly man" was not a new idea. The prophets repeatedly saw visions of God as a man enthroned in the heavens.[4] When Jesus came, He revealed a mystery: God will dwell enthroned in

---

[3] Paul developed this idea from Daniel 7. For more on this, see my book *Son of Man: The Apostles' Gospel*.

[4] Isaiah 6:1; Ezekiel 1:26; Daniel 7:13; Zechariah 3:1–6.

the heavens as a man, *and* He wants a people with Him. The Divine Human is more than God; He is the pattern for a new exalted humanity. He is the "firstborn" of a new humanity.[5]

We are born in Adam's image, but we were always designed to bear the image of the Heavenly Man. Paul repeatedly encouraged the church that anyone who is born again is a "new species" of human joined to the Heavenly Man by the work of the indwelling Spirit.[6] We are "seated" with Him *now* because this was always God's plan. When God made man in His image, He had a specific image in mind, and that image was Himself as a divine human in the person of Jesus.

If we do not become like the Heavenly Man, our lives have been wasted:

> *If in Christ we have hope in this life only, we are of all people most to be pitied. (1 Corinthians 15:19)*

You may have a happy marriage, a stable home, a good job, and integrity, but if you do not live with wisdom and become like the Man in the heavens, it is all a waste. This raises a question: How much time do we spend speaking about the Man in the heavens compared to giving people practical tips for life? The practical tips are helpful but secondary. In fact, they are a pitiful waste of time *if* we do not become like the Man in the heavens.

How much of our preaching and how many of our worship songs reflect Paul's assessment in 1 Corinthians 15:19?

From the very beginning, God intended to dwell in the heavens as an exalted man, so He designed a perfect plan by which He would become a man and then be exalted into the heavens. As we have seen, this age was designed by God to reveal Himself in the person of Jesus *and* exalt Him as a man.[7] Jesus became the Heavenly Man by enduring the suffering of this age, and the same is true for His people.

---

[5] Romans 8:29; 1 Corinthians 15:49; 2 Corinthians 3:18; 4:10–11; 1 John 3:2.

[6] Romans 8:8–9, 11, 15; 1 Corinthians 3:16–17; 2 Corinthians 6:16; Galatians 3:2; 4:6; Ephesians 2:21–22; 5:18; 2 Timothy 1:14

[7] Ephesians 1:10, 20–23; Philippians 2:5–11; Colossians 1:20; Hebrews 1.

We cannot fully comprehend how God produces glory through the hardships of this age or how He advances His purposes through evil actions, but both remain true. God will judge evil and avenge injustice. He cares deeply about the men and spiritual powers that destroy His creation and inflict pain, *and yet* this age is the optimal context to exalt His Son and bring forth His people.

We are accustomed to the idea that this age is a "mistake" that God is trying to "fix," so we struggle to understand that this age was intentional and advances God's purposes, yet the Bible reveals this is true. We should not use this fact to minimize the suffering in this age, but we must know it to give our hearts confidence and courage that, if this age set the stage for Jesus' exaltation, it can do the same for us. If we cooperate with God, He will use this age to make us like the Heavenly Man.

If this age is God's perfect context to reveal and exalt His Son, then it is also the ideal context to form and shape a people into the image of His Son and exalt them with Him.

EMBRACE BIBLICAL DISCIPLESHIP
Discipleship is a seemingly small, tedious, mundane, and sometimes challenging process that will produce a glory beyond everything we can imagine.

As we have seen, God designed this entire age to reveal Himself and produce a people for Himself. Even the evil of this age reveals God in a way that is not otherwise possible. This does not overlook the pain and evil in this age, nor does it excuse the horrendous evil that is done in this age. However, it means that just as God used the darkest evil—the execution of His own Son—to produce and greatest good, He will also use the context of this age to produce a glory in His people that will be similar in nature to what He did for His Son. This does not minimize the scars of evil in this age, but it does give us an unshakable hope. Everything has been made for Jesus. Evil can create great trauma, but it cannot overrule God's purpose for creation.

God created man to experience the revelation of who He is and share in the indescribable pleasure of becoming like Him. Man is capable of carrying God's glory in ways we have not considered or fully understand.[8] Tragically, man is equally capable of profound evil if he does not embrace his calling.

The glory of God's people is veiled because we still live in fallen bodies, but a day is coming when the glory of the new humanity will be fully revealed. When God removes the veil of our sinful flesh and gives us bodies like His, we will shine like the sun. We will be brilliant and dazzling as we reflect God's beauty and glory throughout creation.[9]

The fact God has made His glory full known in a man, Jesus, is an indicator of how much glory He can put in a human.

Every instruction God has given us is designed to prepare us for this glory and exaltation alongside His Son. Jesus specifically asked us to disciple believers to obey *every* command[10] He has given because He knew we tend to overlook the small things we imagine are unimportant:

> *Go therefore and make disciples of all nations . . . teaching them to observe all that I have commanded you. (Matthew 28:19–20)*

We have no idea what is at stake in obeying seemingly small commands of Jesus; therefore, we must give careful attention to the most overlooked commands. Every instruction Jesus has given is for our good. Each one is part of His plan to shape and form us into something glorious that we cannot yet see. Only in the age to come will we fully see what God forms in us through consistent, daily obedience to small instructions throughout our lives.

Do not give up. Do not despise the small things. Resist sin and discouragement with all your might. If you have failed, respond to Him and watch Him produce fruit in your life from your failures. It is never too late to respond to Him.[11] Commit to do the small things well. Far more is at stake than you realize. You are going to be made like Jesus, much more like Him than you can now imagine.

---

[8] 1 Corinthians 2:9; 1 John 3:2.

[9] Romans 8:29; 1 Corinthians 15:49; 2 Corinthians 3:18; 4:10–11; 1 John 3:2.

[10] As a friend once remarked, considering that Jesus is YHWH, "all that I have commanded" is more than Jesus' statement in the Gospels. It comes from everything God has said.

[11] Matthew 21:28–32.

WHERE DID PAUL GET HIS UNDERSTANDING OF GOD'S DESIRE?

Colossians 1 summarizes the divine wisdom that should govern our lives, and Paul's entire life was oriented around this wisdom. Paul's commitment to this wisdom caused him to endure beatings, rejection, and suffering, and to do it all *with joy*. He knew he was living a life of wisdom, and he was certain of God's pleasure over his life.

Paul was tirelessly driven by the vision of a people who would be mature and majestic, a people like Jesus. Paul was confident God would bring this people to maturity, no matter how unlikely it seemed in certain moments. Paul dealt with many challenges in the church. He constantly had to deal with division, pride, racial tension, immorality, betrayal, and suffering, but he had an unshakable conviction that Jesus was going to bring His people to maturity.

Paul's clarity and certainty raise a key question: How did Paul discover the wisdom of God?

Paul was given revelation of a mystery,[12] but the wisdom Paul lived by did not come exclusively from a secret revelation. It came from a key event that occurred just before Jesus' execution. Before Jesus died, Jesus asked His Father for a very specific reward for His suffering. Paul soaked himself in this prayer and committed his life to playing his part to see it answered.

If we want to understand God's wisdom for our lives, we have to know this prayer, and that is where we will turn next.

---

[12] Matthew 13:11; Mark 4:11; Luke 8:10; Romans 16:25; 1 Corinthians 2:7; 4:1; Ephesians 1:9; 3:3–4, 9; 5:32; 6:19; Colossians 1:26–27; 2:2; 4:3; 1 Timothy 3:16.

Will You Respond to Divine Desire?

Jesus' Great Prayer

In eternity past, Jesus chose, as uncreated God and Creator of the cosmos, to become part of His own creation. We will never fully understand what it cost for the Creator of all things to become a creature, but He went far beyond this. Not only did He become a man, He willingly chose to be marred more than any other man[1] and suffer an excruciating death to become a means of salvation for His enemies.

Jesus chose His suffering before He ever became a man, and He lived for approximately thirty-three years knowing His suffering was coming. Every day His suffering came closer, but He did not shrink back. He had made a commitment with Father, and He would keep His commitment.

When the time came, Jesus was overwhelmed but resolute:

And going a little farther he fell on his face and prayed, saying, "My Father, if it be possible, let this cup pass from me; nevertheless, not as I will, but as you will." (Matthew 26:39)

Jesus was overwhelmed by the impending agony, but He remained completely committed to His agreement with the Father. Jesus would fulfill their agreement at the cost of His own life, but He wanted something in return.

Jesus prayed another majestic prayer that night. This prayer is holy ground because it is an intimate conversation between the Father and the Son moments before the Son's horrific suffering began. The prayer reveals the terms of the agreement between the Father and the Son.

---

[1] Isaiah 52:14.

The Son had agreed to suffer because He wanted a reward,[2] and this prayer was a petition for His reward.

This reward is one of the most neglected end-time themes. In fact, the revelation of Jesus is the only end-time theme that is more important than Jesus' reward for His suffering. Many times other end-time themes are given far more emphasis than this theme, and we need to reprioritize our end-time studies according to what Jesus wants from the end times and not what we fear about the end times.

Jesus always gets what He asks the Father for. He fulfilled His part of redemption, and He will be fully rewarded by His Father.

Discipleship is the primary way we partner with the Father in this age to give the Son His reward. The Son's agreement with His Father should undergird our approach to discipleship.

"FATHER, GLORIFY YOUR SON"

Jesus' prayer in John 17 focused in one central reward: *a people*. The prayer opens with Jesus' petition for glory:

> *When Jesus had spoken these words, he lifted up his eyes to heaven, and said, "Father, the hour has come; glorify your Son that the Son may glorify you, since you have given him authority over all flesh, to give eternal life to all whom you have given him. And this is eternal life, that they know you, the only true God, and Jesus Christ whom you have sent." (vv. 1–3)*

This petition is holy. It is not selfish in any way because Jesus wants to magnify His Father by using His divine cosmic authority to give eternal life to a people so they can know the Father and Son.

The word *know* in English does not adequately convey the request. This was not a request to share information. It was a request to give the power of eternal life to a people so they could enter into the divine fellowship of the Godhead.[3] This "knowledge" is an intimate and relational knowledge, the same kind of knowledge the Father and Son have of each other. The idea that fallen humans can enter into deep fellowship with the Godhead is unthinkable, and yet this is what Jesus wants from His Father as a reward for His suffering.

---

[2]John 17; Hebrews 12:2.

[3]George R. Beasley-Murray, *John*, vol. 36, Word Biblical Commentary (Dallas: Word, Incorporated, 1999), 297.

On the night of His betrayal, Jesus' asked His Father for the glory necessary to give a people indestructible life so they could enter deep and everlasting fellowship with the Godhead. Jesus wants to be glorified, and His glory is connected to a glorified people.

Jesus did not suffer for the sake of suffering; Jesus embraced the cross so He could receive a great reward and secure eternal life for a people. Jesus' glory was deeply connected to His cross, and the same is true for us. Jesus' invitation to take up our own cross and follow Him is not primarily a call to hardship. It is a call to a narrow path of self-denial to inherit a glory that cannot come any other way.

As the prayer unfolded, Jesus continued His focus on a people:

I have manifested your name to the people whom you gave me out of the world. Yours they were, and you gave them to me, and they have kept your word. (v. 6)

I am praying for them. I am not praying for the world but for those whom you have given me, for they are yours. All mine are yours, and yours are mine. (vv. 9–10)

This part of the prayer contains an astounding revelation: *The people the Father gave to Jesus also belong to the Father.* The Father gave them to Jesus as a gift, but Jesus gave them back to the Father saying, *"All mine are yours, and yours are mine."* Jesus knew the Father wanted a people, so He appealed to the Father's desire for a people, knowing He was asking for exactly what the Father wanted.

Jesus essentially said, "Father, We both deeply desire a people, so give Me the glory necessary to secure the people We desire. If You give Me glory, I will use it to produce a people and give them to You. We will both get what We want—a people who have deep communion with both of Us. I know how deeply You desire this, so I will endure unprecedented suffering to redeem them and make them compatible to Us."

There are innumerable ways for Jesus to be glorified, but Jesus chose *one* demonstration to stand above all others: *He wanted to be glorified in a people:*

I am glorified in them. (v. 10)

69 What Does God Want?

Jesus' suffering is an incomparable act that will reverberate throughout all eternity. No other man could have suffered the way Jesus suffered. Because Jesus' suffering is unparalleled, it deserves the highest honor and the maximum glory. *Jesus asked to be glorified in a people as the highest reward He could receive—the thing that would best demonstrate His matchless splendor.*

Not only will this people magnify Jesus, they will fill Him with deep delight:

> *But now I am coming to you, and these things I speak in the world, that they may have my joy fulfilled in themselves. (v. 13)*

Jesus is the most joyful man that has ever lived,[4] but His joy is incomplete until He receives the reward of His people. They will glorify and delight Jesus in a way nothing else in creation can, and if we care about Jesus' pleasure, we will invest our lives in the church to play our part to see Him receive His reward.

Jesus' joy is in a people like Him who will become a corporate bride. He has been living with incomplete joy for thousands of years, but a day is coming when His joy will be fulfilled.

Jesus knew how much the Father longed for this people, so He set Himself apart as a sacrifice and prepared for death to purchase what the Father wanted:[5]

> *And for their sake I consecrate myself. (v. 19)*

Jesus knew the Father's desire for this people was so strong it was worth His death and permanent disfigurement.

Jesus loved His first disciples deeply, but they were not His entire reward. He asked the Father for a much bigger people:

> *I do not ask for these only, but also for those who will believe in me through their word . . . that they also may be in us. (vv. 20–21)*

---

[4] Psalm 45:7; Hebrews 1:9.

[5] We think of consecration as an individual act, but Jesus consecrated Himself for the sake of His people. Our consecration should also be for benefit of the body, not our own personal piety.

Jesus asked the Father for us as a reward! Jesus prayed that we *all* would enter into the fellowship of the Godhead. This is an unthinkable exaltation. It is an exaltation into the Godhead without becoming God. Do you realize that Jesus asked the Father to bring *you* into intimate communion with the Godhead?

Jesus loved His first disciples deeply, but He prayed for every one of His disciples—even those born two thousand years later. You did not receive the privilege of following Jesus in ancient Israel, but you are still precious to Jesus. You are not second class. Jesus prayed for you and asked the Father to exalt you and bring you into Their communion. *And Jesus gets what He wants.*

JESUS' PEOPLE

The ancient world did not have big fonts or bold letters, so its people used repetition to emphasize things. As I noted before, whenever you see repetition, especially what is in close proximity, it is the equivalent of bold text or a person raising their voice. Repetition, then, is making a big point that we are supposed to notice. For example, many of Jesus' teachings begin with "Truly, truly," but Jesus probably did not say truly twice. It is more likely He raised His voice and spoke the word with strength. When Jesus repeats something, He wants you to pay close attention to it, and He repeated several things about His people.

Jesus' people are not of this world, just as He is not of this world. Jesus referred to the world eighteen times in thirteen verses and six times in three verses in John 17:

> *I have given them your word, and the world has hated them because they are not of the world, just as I am not of the world. I do not ask that you take them out of the world, but that you keep them from the evil one. They are not of the world, just as I am not of the world.* (vv. 14–16)

Jesus' people are like Him because they belong to Him. Like Him, they do not live according to the systems of this age. They love like Him, think like Him, speak like Him, live like Him, and will be treated as He was treated. They are a corporate witness of Jesus in this age, living as He lived. If the people of this age find us "normal" and we do not stick out in any way, we are not living according to who we are.

Jesus' people are set apart just as He is set apart. Jesus consecrated (dedicated) Himself to God's service in order to sanctify a people:

> *Sanctify them in the truth; your word is truth. As you sent me into the world, so I have sent them into the world. And for their sake I consecrate myself, that they also may be sanctified in truth. (vv. 17–19)*

The words *consecrated* and *sanctified* both come from the same Greek word. Jesus set Himself apart in a unique way so we could become set apart as He is.

Jesus made three main requests up to this point:

- He wanted to be glorified.
- He wanted a reward for His suffering.
- He wanted His joy to be complete.

All of these requests are answered by a people.

A CORPORATE WITNESS OF JESUS

Jesus concluded His prayer by making some of the most significant statements He ever made about His people. Again, Jesus repeated Himself a number of times to emphasize just how important each part of His request was to Him.

> *I do not ask for these only, but also for those who will believe in me through their word, that they may all be one, just as you, Father, are in me, and I in you, that they also may be in us, so that the world may believe that you have sent me. (vv. 20–21)*

Jesus prayed that His people would be "one," which He describes as the deep unity like the unity He has with His Father. Jesus asked the Father to make this people one so they can be joined to the Trinity and enter into the kind of communion Jesus has with the Father.

Do you realize Jesus prayed that we would have the kind of communion with Him and the Father that He had with the Father as a man?

I must emphasize that this does not mean we will become divine, but I also must stress that Jesus asked the Father to unify His people so we can interact with the Trinity the way Jesus interacts with His Father. Jesus' request is completely outrageous, but He gets everything He asked His Father for. This request is so unthinkable that it is easy for us not to take it seriously and assume it refers to some time in the distant future when we are with God in "heaven,"[6] but that is simply not true. We must read Jesus' prayer carefully and slowly.

Jesus asked the Father to form a unified people and bring them "into" the Godhead so that the world will believe He was sent by the Father.

Notice Jesus asked the Father to fulfill this prayer in this age *before* His return to give a witness to the world in this age. When Jesus returns, the nations will see His glory,[7] and He will not need another witness to demonstrate to the world who He is. When the world sees Him descending from heaven, there will be no question about His identity.

Right now, Jesus is absent, and He wants a witness in the earth who provides indisputable evidence He is the Divine Human who has descended and ascended. This people must be revealed in the sight of the world *before* Jesus' return. They will be a sign and a wonder because they are a unified people—one just as the Trinity is one.

Unity does not mean uniformity, and therein lies the wonder of this people. The Trinity is unified, but it is distinct. The Father, Son, and Spirit have distinctions. They are not identical, and the same will be true of this people. They will retain all sorts of diversity but have an intense love for each other. They will honor and submit to each other. They will break down the ancient animosity between races and cultures and become a flesh-and-blood demonstration of the nature of the Trinity. If this people all share the same background, their unity is not miraculous, showing this will be a diverse yet distinct people coming out of every race and culture.[8]

This people will be in communion with the Trinity to the same degree Jesus was during His earthly ministry. They will live in communion with the Father, as Jesus does in this age. When others encounter this people, they will encounter a demonstration of Jesus and be convinced Jesus is precisely who He said He was.

---

[6]It is worth noting the Bible never predicts the saints will dwell in "heaven" in eternity. The Bible predicts God will dwell with man on the earth.

[7]Matthew 16:27; 24:30; 2 Thessalonians 1:7–9; Jude 14–15; Revelation 19:1, 11–12.

[8]It will be the ultimate fulfillment of Genesis 12:3. For more on this, see my books, *One King* and *It Must Be Finished*.

73 What Does God Want?

Have you considered that, before the age is finished, the church will be the primary witness of Jesus—indisputable evidence He exists?

If you ask people what the primary evidence of the gospel is, you will probably get several answers such as:

- The Bible.
- The historical evidence for the resurrection.
- The testimony of creation.
- The ongoing witness of Israel.

These are all good answers, but they are not the answer Jesus gave. For example, He did not say, "The world will believe I was sent because of what is in the Bible," though the Bible is a testimony of Jesus. He predicted the church would become the primary evidence of the gospel. The world will be unable to deny Jesus when it encounters His people in this age *before* Jesus returns.

This seems impossible, and it is easy to be discouraged by the weakness of the church. However, do you have more confidence in your perception about the church than what Jesus asked His Father to do for Him? Most of us put more weight on what we see than what Jesus said, and this must change. When we put confidence in our doubts, we hinder the purposes of God, but when we put all our trust in what Jesus asked for, we will cooperate with God to bring it to pass.

The church will be fully human, still in fallen bodies and yet in intimate communion with the Trinity, and a corporate demonstration of Jesus. This is especially phenomenal considering it must occur before we are given glorified bodies. Jesus is going to produce an indisputable witness of His glory in our weakness. Individually, we will not be noteworthy, but as a people we will be stunning. This is completely impossible by any human means, which is why it will be an indisputable witness of Jesus.

Jesus began the conclusion to His prayer by focusing on an incredible theme: a people who will be His primary witness in this age. We need to note a few things in His prayer up to this point:

- Jesus is leaving the world, so it will not have a physical witness of Him.

- Jesus is going to leave a people in the world. He will be in this people, and they will be so much like Him that they will be a witness to the world which it cannot deny.
- Jesus was a physical manifestation of God, and His people will also be a manifestation of God in this age (though they will not become divine).
- This people will be brought into the Trinity in fellowship. Their communion with the Trinity will be like Jesus' communion with His Father.
- This people will have distinctions yet be unified as a corporate people. God is the model for this people, and they will resemble the Trinity.
- This people must emerge before Jesus' return.

Jesus was not finished yet. He had more to say about this people.

A People with Jesus' Glory

Not only will Jesus bring a people into fellowship with the Trinity, He has also given them His glory:

> *The glory that you have given me I have given to them, that they may be one even as we are one, I in them and you in me, that they may become perfectly one, so that the world may know that you sent me and loved them even as you loved me. (John 17:22–23)*

Jesus has given His people His glory so they become one people like the Trinity. We see again why Paul said the mystery of Christ is revealed in a unified people. *If we perceive this aspect of Jesus' glory, we will work tirelessly for unity in the body across racial, ethnic, and social divisions.*

The beginning of John's gospel helps us better understand this part of the prayer:

> *In the beginning was the Word, and the Word was with God, and the Word was God. He was in the beginning with God. All things were made through him, and without him was not any thing made that was made. In him was life, and the life was the light of men. The light shines in the darkness, and the darkness has not overcome it. (John 1:1–5)*

> *And the Word became flesh and dwelt among us, and we have seen his glory, glory as of the only Son from the Father, full of grace and truth. (v. 14)*

When Jesus took on flesh, the world saw the unique glory of God in the person of Jesus, and it was like a divine shaft of light shattering the darkness. God had revealed His mystery: He would reveal Himself most completely in a human. This witness began with Jesus, and it did not end with Jesus' ascension. God continues to give a witness of

Himself in human form through a people who have been given His own glory.

Jesus does not possess an independent glory. His glory is inseparable from His relationship with His Father and the Spirit. In the same way, Jesus gave His glory to a corporate people who are connected to each other so deeply they are becoming "perfectly one"—a people who resemble the Trinity. They are distinct and yet one. This is the only way we will experience what Jesus has given His people and the only way the world will see a manifestation of that glory.

Jesus did not give His glory to us as individuals, nor did He give it to a people who may identify with each other but remain very independent.

UNDENIABLE EVIDENCE OF THE DIVINE HUMAN

Do we realize what is at stake in the corporate people of God? According to Jesus, the church has been given His own glory to become the visible, undeniable evidence of the incarnation. In the church, the world will see a glimpse of God through humanity.

In verse 23, Jesus asked a second time that His people would be His primary witness to the world:

> *That they may all be one, just as you, Father, are in me, and I in you, that they also may be in us, so that the world may believe that you have sent me. . . . I in them and you in me, that they may become perfectly one, so that the world may know that you sent me and loved them even as you loved me. (John 17:21, 23)*

Jesus' repetition confronts our view of the church: *Do we see the church the way Jesus did?* Do we really believe that the people of God are the primary evidence of Jesus in this age? Do we have Jesus' vision for the church? Do we really believe God is building a church that provides the world with a glimpse of God revealed through a corporate people—and that this glimpse is so profound it forces the world to acknowledge God has come as a man?

In both verses, Jesus asked the Father to make the church His witness, but He changed one word in the second request:

> *so that the world may* believe *that you have sent me. (John 17:21 emphasis added)*

so that the world may know *that you sent me. (John 17:23 emphasis added)*

In His first request, Jesus asked the Father to make His people one so the world would *believe* the Father had sent Him. Jesus used the word *pisteuō* (πιστεύω), which carries the idea of believing something is true and putting your trust in it. This word is used throughout the New Testament for people who believe in Jesus, and in verse 21 Jesus asked the Father for a church that will cause the world to put its trust in Him unto salvation.

In His second request, Jesus asked the Father to give His glory to His people and make them one so the world would *know* the Father had sent Him. Jesus used the word *ginōskō* (γινώσκω), which essentially means to know or acknowledge.[1] The word indicates something is known or understood by acquiring information or by experience, but it does not carry the sense of believing faith or trust.

The two requests are nearly identical, but the difference in one word reveals Jesus has two purposes in mind for His people. He first asked the Father to make His people a demonstration that would cause the world to "believe" and put its trust in Him. Jesus wanted the world to see a witness in His people that provoked it to put its trust in Him and become part of His people. The first witness is a salvific witness—an act of evangelism.

The second witness is different from the first one. In His second request, Jesus asked the Father to give the world a demonstration of His glory in His people that would require the world to acknowledge He had been sent by the Father. This witness is different because it may or may not cause the world to put its faith in Jesus, but it will force the world to acknowledge Jesus is alive and is the Divine Human.

Jesus asked for both witnesses, and He will get them. Many will be drawn to the church when they see the nature of Jesus expressed among His people. Others will not be drawn to the church, but they will see the glory of Jesus and the witness of His nature among a people and be forced to acknowledge that Jesus is the Divine Human sent by the Father.

---

[1] Johannes P. Louw and Eugene Albert Nida, *Greek-English Lexicon of the New Testament: Based on Semantic Domains* (New York: United Bible Societies, 1996), 368.

THE UNFOLDING WITNESS

The witness Jesus prayed for is an unfolding witness. It has happened through history, but it will also climax in a witness given at the end of the age just before Jesus returns. The end of the age will climax in the revelation of Jesus in His return, but as we have already seen, there will also be an unprecedented revelation of Jesus through His people.

Because Jesus' people are a witness of Him, their witness to Him will unfold over time in a way that is very similar to the way Jesus' life unfolded. Every part of His life was a witness to the Father, but there was a clear progression in His life. The corporate witness of Jesus through His people will follow a similar progression. The pattern of Jesus' life is not a precise formula, but it does give us insight into God's plan for His people:

- For the first thirty years, Jesus gave a witness to the Father in the mundane tasks of daily life. He steadily grew in wisdom and stature. He lived a life of faithfulness and service in a small place, revealing the deep humility of God and God's great delight in the things we consider small.

- For three years, Jesus had a public ministry with His disciples. He was much more visible during these three years teaching and healing. He began empowering His disciples and sending them out, and He interacted with a wide number of people from various backgrounds.

- For a little over three days, Jesus gave the most astounding revelation of God in His earthly ministry. He was betrayed, willingly suffered, was publicly executed, and then suddenly resurrected. It was an unparalleled revelation of God and glorified Jesus in a specific way.

- Jesus' witness concluded with His ascension into the heavens to take His place as the exalted Divine Human.

Jesus gave a profound revelation of the Father that unfolded over time and grew in intensity. The most intense revelation of God's nature unfolded in just over three days during the most dramatic events of Jesus' ministry. The church is a corporate revelation of Jesus, and we should expect the revelation of Jesus through His people to unfold in a similar way:

- The church began in a small place and has steadily grown over time. For most of church history, the church has not been a global influence, but the true church has been a witness of Jesus wherever she was.[2]
- In the last century or so, the church has quickly become much more visible. The gospel has expanded throughout the world, and access to the Bible is now much more widespread than it was for the majority of history.[3]
- The Bible predicts the age will end in a brief time of unprecedented trouble that lasts approximately three and a half years.[4] During this time, the church will pass through unprecedented trouble, and that trouble will produce an unprecedented witness of Jesus. Just as God was revealed most deeply in Jesus' suffering, so Jesus will be be revealed most deeply through His people in the final years of this age.
- At the return of Jesus, the church will be caught up into the heavens to take an exalted place with Jesus.[5]

The witness of Jesus through His people has been unfolding throughout history, and it is building up to a grand climax.

The final moments of Jesus' ministry give us a preview of the final years of this age. Jesus' glory is connected to His suffering, death, and resurrection, and He has given that glory to His people. Therefore, we should expect His glory to be most intensely revealed through His people in the last moments of the age, which mirror Jesus' own suffering.

Jesus walked through a prototype of the end-time drama in His ministry, suffering, and victorious resurrection. He endured incredible

---

[2] I am not including the political entity typically referred to as "Christendom" as part of this witness because of the mixture involved. Christendom was bold and public but not the embodied witness Jesus asked for.

[3] While access to the gospel has exploded in the last century, it is important to remember that nearly two billion people have still not heard the gospel.

[4] Daniel 7:25; 9:27; 12:7; Revelation 11:2–3; 13:5.

[5] 1 Thessalonians 4:16–17.

tribulation and secured the salvation of God, but He did not fulfill everything the prophets predicted.[6] The outpouring of the Spirit and the miracles that accompanied Jesus' ministry and His victory were all foreshadowings of the ultimate fulfillment of God's promises when the Spirit is poured out on all flesh, the knowledge of God covers the earth, and God restores all things.[7]

The victory of God is already breaking into this age, but everything has not yet been fulfilled.

Jesus' glory was veiled by His own human body, and He was mocked as just another human because He seemed too ordinary. For years, Jesus seemed too "normal," and when His glory was revealed, people were shocked and appalled. As Jesus hung exposed on the cross, a glory that had been partially veiled for thousands of years was suddenly and publicly uncovered, and it was radically different from every human definition of glory.

What happened to Jesus will happen to the church.

Glimpses of the glory of the church have been seen throughout history, but the true glory of the church is largely hidden. Like Jesus, the church seems incredibly ordinary because she consists of humans. The weakness of humanity veils the glory of the church just as it veiled Jesus' glory.[8] Jesus' ordinary appearance caused people to treat Him with contempt, and we need to be careful not to treat the seemingly ordinary church with the same contempt.

A day is coming when God will suddenly reveal His church just before Jesus returns. God will suddenly expose and uncover His church just as His Son was exposed in His suffering. The glory of the church will be made known publicly in a way it has not been before. To the world, it will seem to be a moment of humiliation and suffering. However, it will be a sudden revelation of who the church truly is—a people who share Jesus' glory.

---

[6] Acts 1:6–8; 3:19–21.

[7] Psalm 67:2; 72:19; 98:1–3; 102:25–26; Isaiah 6:3; 11:9; 32:15; 44:3–5; 65:17; Ezekiel 36:25–27; 39:29; Joel 2:28; Habakkuk 2:14; Romans 8:20–21; 2 Peter 3:10–13; Revelation 21–22.

[8] Romans 8:3.

The true church has been a beautiful demonstration of Jesus through history, and she will follow the complete pattern of Jesus' life. There is a witness coming that will cause the entire world—those who believe and those who do not—to know beyond a shadow of a doubt Jesus is the Divine Human sent by the Father. The "body" of Jesus will reflect His glory.

We need a confident expectation that Jesus is going to reveal His own glory through His people in a way we cannot fully anticipate. This anticipation should fuel our discipleship.

We do not know what generation will give this witness. Perhaps our generation will live through the final trouble, or perhaps a generation after ours will. Regardless of when this demonstration comes, we are part of a corporate people connected across the generations.

Abraham's faithfulness was critical for the blessings we now enjoy,[9] and in the same way our labor in faithful discipleship will play a role in the maturing of the church whether God finishes the age in our lifetime or not. Jesus lived in obscurity for thirty years and ministered publicly for three years to prepare Him to reveal God in an unequaled way in a little over three days. The life of the church in this age is also preparing for an unprecedented witness of Jesus through His people.

The glory of God was revealed through every moment of Jesus' first coming, but it led to a moment when God was revealed in a way that was shocking, completely unanticipated, and glorious beyond measure. The same will be true of the church.

LOVED LIKE JESUS

Jesus wants His people to become living evidence that the Father loves His people *just as He loves Jesus:*

> *I in them and you in me, that they may become perfectly one, so that the world may know that you sent me and loved them even as you loved me. (John 17:23)*

This is a profound glimpse into the Father's desire for a people. Jesus and the Father *both* love Their people in the most intense way that God can love another person. The Father's love for His people is so strong

---

[9] Hebrews 11:39–12:2.

Jesus ended the prayer with a final request for the Father's love to dwell in His people.

> *I made known to them your name, and I will continue to make it known, that the love with which you have loved me may be in them, and I in them. (v. 26)*

Jesus' prayer reveals the church is not just the Bride of Jesus; she is the desire of the Godhead. Jesus secured our access to the Godhead where we commune with the Father and the Son by the Spirit. The Son's communion with the Father and Their relationship of love are the prototype of our relationship with Them in the Godhead.[10]

Do we love the church the way the Father does?

The Father longs for a unified people—one new man—from the nations. Before the age ends, the Father will demonstrate His affection for this people in an extravagant way, and the world will *know* the Father loves this people with the same intensity He loves Jesus. When we wholeheartedly engage in discipleship, we not only give Jesus what He wants, we also give the Father what He wants.

Before the age is over, the world will know and acknowledge that the Father loves His people just as He loves His Son.

If the Father loves His people the way He loves His Son, we should expect Him to lead His people the way He led Jesus. He will also glorify the church the way He has glorified Jesus. His leadership can be perplexing, but it is designed to secure a glory we cannot imagine through a process we do not fully anticipate.

"FATHER, I DESIRE"

Jesus concluded His prayer by asking the Father for His people to encounter His glory:

> *Father, I desire that they also, whom you have given me, may be with me where I am, to see my glory that you have given me because you loved me before the foundation of the world. (v. 24)*

Can you imagine the response in the heart of God any time Jesus says, "Father, I desire . . . "? The Father will not deny His Son. He will fulfill

---

[10] I use the phrase, "in the Godhead," not to say humans will be divine, but because this is the language Jesus used in His prayer.

every longing in His Son's heart because the Son's desires are the Father's desires.

Jesus wants His people with Him, and He wants His people to see His glory. Jesus' deepest longings are unveiled in His desire for nearness with His people. He wants them *with Him*. He wants intimate communion and physical nearness. He is not looking for more servants or distant managers. He wants something more—He wants a people who are with Him.

Jesus wants His people to see His glory which is a reference back to His request in verse 22. If we put the two verses together, we can better understand what Jesus wants:

> *The glory that you have given me I have given to them. . . . Father, I desire that they also, whom you have given me, may be with me where I am, to see my glory that you have given me because you loved me before the foundation of the world. (vv. 22, 24)*

Jesus wants His people to see His glory so they will know the glory He has shared with them. *His glory is our glory.* To use an analogy, this is like a husband revealing the full extent of his wealth to his new bride to show her what now belongs to her. Jesus wants us to behold His glory so we will know what belongs to us in Him. As we see His glory, we begin to enjoy what it means to belong to Him, and we can live in light of His glory. *In the process, we become the fulfillment of divine desire.*

IMPLICATIONS OF JOHN 17

In John 17, Jesus expressed the eternal longing of God. In that holy moment, the disciples heard the Son speak to the Father about the dream of Their heart that led Them to create the cosmos and set the plan of redemption into motion. This dream was so precious to Them it was worth the Son becoming a man, suffering intensely, and even enduring death. John presents this as the grand conclusion of Jesus' ministry. After this prayer, Jesus went to the cross to secure the answer to His prayer.

Jesus embraced the agony of the cross for the joy set before Him, and John 17 reveals that joy.

> *Looking to Jesus, the founder and perfecter of our faith, who for the joy that was set before him endured the cross, despising the shame, and is seated at the right hand of the throne of God. (Hebrews 12:2)*

Jesus prayed with absolute certainty that the Father would answer His prayer. He knew the joy He would receive, and before His suffering began, He expressed His desire to His Father. John 17 is a holy contract between the Father and the Son, summarizing what the Son wanted in reward for His suffering. The Son asked for His reward with great delight because He knew the joy set before Him was also the deepest longing of the Father's heart.

Jesus' prayer developed God's two purposes for this age.

Jesus expressed God's desire to make Himself known:

> *And this is eternal life, that they know you, the only true God, and Jesus Christ whom you have sent. I glorified you on earth. . . . I have manifested your name to the people whom you gave me out of the world. . . . For I have given them the words that you gave me, and they have received them and have come to know in truth that I came from you; and they have*

> *believed that you sent me. . . . I have given them your word, and the world has hated them because they are not of the world, just as I am not of the world. The glory that you have given me I have given to them. . . . Father, I desire that they also, whom you have given me, may be with me where I am, to see my glory that you have given me because you loved me before the foundation of the world. . . . I made known to them your name, and I will continue to make it known. (vv. 3–4, 6, 8, 14, 22, 24, 26)*

Jesus expressed God's desire to form a people for Himself who are like Him:

> *You have given him authority over all flesh, to give eternal life to all whom you have given him. And this is eternal life, that they know you, the only true God, and Jesus Christ whom you have sent. . . . I have manifested your name to the people whom you gave me out of the world. Yours they were, and you gave them to me, and they have kept your word. Now they know that everything that you have given me is from you. For I have given them the words that you gave me, and they have received them and have come to know in truth that I came from you; and they have believed that you sent me. I am praying for them. I am not praying for the world but for those whom you have given me, for they are yours. All mine are yours, and yours are mine, and I am glorified in them. And I am no longer in the world, but they are in the world, and I am coming to you. Holy Father, keep them in your name, which you have given me, that they may be one, even as we are one. While I was with them, I kept them in your name. . . . But now I am coming to you, and these things I speak in the world, that they may have my joy fulfilled in themselves. I have given them your word, and the world has hated them because they are not of the world, just as I am not of the world. I do not ask that you take them out of the world, but that you keep them from the evil one. They are not of the world, just as I am not of the world. Sanctify them in the truth; your word is truth. As you sent me into the world, so I have sent them into the world. And for their sake I consecrate myself, that they also may be sanctified in truth. I do not ask for these only, but also for those who will believe in me through their word, that they may all be one, just as you, Father, are in me, and I in you, that they also may be in us, so that the world may believe that you have sent me. The glory that you have given me I have given to them, that they may be one even as we are one, I in them and you in me, that they may become perfectly one, so that the world may*

know that you sent me and loved them even as you loved me. Father, I desire that they also, whom you have given me, may be with me where I am, to see my glory that you have given me because you loved me before the foundation of the world. . . . I made known to them your name, and I will continue to make it known, that the love with which you have loved me may be in them, and I in them. (vv. 2–3, 6–24, 26)

As Jesus prayed, God's two purposes came together. Jesus asked the Father to reveal Him to the world through His people:

That they may all be one, just as you, Father, are in me, and I in you, that they also may be in us, so that the world may believe that you have sent me. . . . I in them and you in me, that they may become perfectly one, so that the world may know that you sent me and loved them even as you loved me. (vv. 21–23)

God's two purposes drive everything He does in this age, and these two purposes are deeply intertwined.

THE CROSS WAS MORE THAN FORGIVENESS

The forgiveness secured by the cross is beautiful and precious, but if we reduce the gospel to forgiveness, our gospel is incomplete. Jesus purchased our mercy to secure something glorious and to enable His people to become what He and the Father want.

Jesus died to create a "new species" of human.[1] The Trinity has dreamed of this new humanity from the very beginning. Jesus is the firstborn brother of this new humanity, and we are made like Him. The new humanity is a demonstration of Jesus because we are still human but have God's divine life dwelling in us. Jesus alone is the full demonstration of God, but each new human is a partial yet authentic demonstration of Him. We have not yet received redeemed bodies, but the inner transformation that has begun in us by the Spirit enables us to become His living witnesses.

The church is a witness of the new humanity—a demonstration that Jesus is real and a revelation of what He wants man to be. Discipleship is the process that matures this witness.

---

[1] Romans 8:29; 1 Corinthians 15:49; 2 Corinthians 3:18; 4:10–11; 1 John 3:2.

When Jesus uttered the words, *"Father, I desire,"* as a divine human, He expressed the motivation behind all creation. He used words to speak the ache of the Creator: *"I want a people with Me where I am. I want a people like Me. Father, give Us a people."*

The story of redemption is not primarily a story of "restoration." God is not bringing humanity back to the Garden of Eden nor trying to make us into the Adam's image. God is forming a new humanity in the image of a new "Adam,"[2] and we are destined for a new creation. God's plan is forward looking, not backward looking. Though this age began with man's sin, it will fulfill God's deepest longing. Human sin and the rebellion of the powers brought great destruction into God's creation, but ironically it is going to ultimately produce what God wanted from the beginning.

We deal with the effects of sin every day, so it's difficult to see what God is doing, but something spectacular is underway. God is remaking the world in the most shocking way. He is working through His executed Son to produce a people who will be shaped and formed by following the path Jesus took for His own exaltation.[3] They endure the suffering, sin, and death of this age, and the Father is using it to transform them into the likeness of His Son.

In our time, the gospel is often preached as an invitation to repent so that we can be right with God as individuals. Our personal relationships with Jesus are critical, but they are not the full gospel. When they become the entire gospel, it obscures God's full purpose. The gospel is an invitation to repent so that we can be right with God *and* become part of the people who are right with God. We must be born again personally, and that personal transformation enables us to become part of a people and not merely live a life of private devotion on our own.

The apostles called men to repent so they could become part of the people of God.

Private devotion is important, but it is one component of our discipleship. To come to maturity, we must become part of the corporate body. There are things God will never address personally to

---

[2] 1 Corinthians 15:45–49.

[3] Matthew 10:38–39; 16:24–26; Mark 8:34–35; Luke 9:23–26; 14:27.

us because He did not design us to mature as isolated individuals. There are some things in your life that God will address through your relationship with the body. Other believers will have insights that the Lord will use to mature you as you interact with the body.

Some people are hoping to become a "super saint" who reveals all the facets of the beauty of Jesus. People should encounter Jesus in you as an individual, but Jesus is the only individual who is a full manifestation of God. God will not give you all His gifts.[4] However, God does give all the gifts of His Spirit to a corporate people. That corporate people then become a demonstration of the beauty of Jesus. As individual followers of Jesus are formed into a people, they become a demonstration that is much greater than any single member.

As individuals, we each have real weaknesses.[5] We try to avoid weakness because we long to be confident and strong, but strength fuels pride, and God resists it.[6] Strength is found when weak people come together as one corporate people. God releases His strength on the body in a way that does not fuel pride or exalt any specific person, but instead exalts His Son.

When this age is finished, we will not be amazed by our own strength. We will be awed at what Jesus has accomplished through a people who embraced their own weaknesses so the power of Jesus could be manifested in them. The power of God can flow through weakness in a way that it cannot flow through strength. As long as we seek our own strength and our own exaltation, we will not fully experience the power of God. When we become weak enough, though, God will release something through His people that we cannot now imagine. That power will not fully come on individuals; it will come upon a people and glorify the God who gave it.

---

[4]Romans 12:6; 1 Corinthians 12:11–30; Ephesians 4:7.

[5]Weakness is very different from compromise. Weakness is the lack of power and strength. Our weakness is not sin, and we must be patient with our weakness and the weakness of others. Compromise is agreement with sin and disagreement with God's ways in our own personal lives. We must resist compromise.

[6]Psalm 138:6; Proverbs 3:34; 15:33; 18:12; 22:4; Isaiah 57:15; Matthew 23:12; 1 Peter 5:5; James 4:6.

A People like Jesus

Jesus is not looking for people who can follow a certain set of rules. For example, Jesus did not serve because it was the right thing to do—He served because He *enjoys* serving. In many cases, we try to get people to imitate the behavior of Jesus, but Jesus wants people to love what He loves.

Changed behavior is the fruit of discipleship, but not the central goal.

The goal of discipleship is the transformation of a people into the image of Jesus. It is important to stop sinful behaviors and to embrace helpful disciplines, but changed behavior is not the indicator that a person is discipled. The real indicator is changed affections. There are many ways for humans to make significant changes in their behavior, but discipleship transforms the affections of a people. Changed behavior can (and should) be an evidence of new affections,[7] but it is possible for behavior to change without affections changing.

God wants a people who are like Him, not a people who try to act like Him.

How many of our messages teach people how to act instead of teaching people the knowledge of God, calling them to embrace the path of becoming like Him? It is possible to be honest at work, have a good marriage, and a stable home life, and not truly love God or His ways.

When we reduce God to a moral code, we do not disciple people; we deceive them. We convince them that they are something they are not.

God's desire for a people who want to be like Him and not simply follow a moral code explains the unusual ways He relates to people. For example, God deeply loved David, even though David was guilty of serious sins and had many failures. Though David's failures were serious, David also had a deep longing to be made like God. He truly loved what he saw about God. God responded to this desire and remained deeply committed to David throughout His failures.

On the other hand, Jesus had profound trouble with many religious leaders. These leaders all had much better outward behavior than David, and they kept the law carefully. They embraced religious rules, but they did not truly embrace God and, as a result, strongly opposed Jesus.

---

[7]Matthew 3:7–10; Ephesians 2:10; 1 Timothy 4:8; Titus 1:16; 3:8; James 1:22–25; 2:14–26.

ALIGNING WITH GOD'S PURPOSES

When we consider Jesus' prayer, it tells us several things about God's purposes for the church:

- Jesus is the only Human who contains the fullness of God, but He is forming a people who are also filled with God and reveal God to the world around them. Jesus has given this task to a corporate people and not to individuals, because He is the only individual who can reveal the fullness of God. When we read this individualistically, we put unnecessary pressure on ourselves and others (especially leaders).

- God distributes His attributes and likeness among His people. When everyone in the community contributes their part, a corporate entity emerges which demonstrates the nature of God. The corporate calling on the church to demonstrate the nature of God requires every individual to contribute from the grace of God given to them.

- We have been given the Holy Spirit to become a corporate demonstration of Jesus, a "new species" of humanity. This new humanity is modeled after Jesus. Jesus is unique because He is God living in a human frame, and this is precisely what the Holy Spirit does in us. When we are born again, we are remade as humans with God dwelling inside. Unlike Jesus, we do not become divine, but God dwells in our human frames, making us like Jesus and as close to God as a creature can be.

- If you want to become like Jesus, you must be in the community. You will find Jesus *in the community*. The community is also the context for you to begin living as Jesus. Jesus lived within community His entire life. He was in perfect union with His Father and the Spirit. This union in community enabled Him to be the full manifestation of God. Our union with each other by the Spirit will also enable us to become a manifestation of Jesus.

- Jesus has set His community in the world to function as He did. We are a corporate expression of the person of Jesus. This corporate expression of Jesus must come to maturity before

He returns because this people is His Bride. His Bride will be compatible to Him and will be His eternal companion.

- The church is sent into the world as Jesus was sent. The sending of Jesus is what made God known. Without that, we had an incomplete view of God. Jesus sent a community. That implies this community makes God known. *When this community is not what God intends, God is not made known in the way He wants to be made known.* Again, we see why Paul had such zeal for the community. The "one new man" is a corporate Jesus (though not divine) and, therefore, has to resemble Jesus in all the ways God intended so that the nations will know who God is.

- Jesus revealed the nature of God within the limitations of the fallen body Mary gave Him.[8] While Jesus was completely sinless, He lived in a body like ours as a prototype of His purposes for this age. Through the Spirit, He will reveal the knowledge of God through His people in this age before they receive new bodies.

Do your hopes, dreams, goals, plans, and daily schedule align with these purposes?

---

[8]Romans 8:3.

I Want a People

The entire story of redemption is shaped by God's desire for a people, and the New Testament contains the open mystery of what that people are like and how God is going to produce them.

An idol is a physical representation of a god. It is not the god. Man is the image and representation of God in creation, and there is a sense in which man is presented in the Old Testament as God's "idol."[1] God forbids idols because He cannot be accurately expressed by anything we can make *and* because God has already provided His own image: man.

Jesus is the premier human image of God and the only complete image of God fully expressed in a man. Jesus will always be supreme because He alone *is* God, but He is also the first of a company of humans who will demonstrate God's image as well. Jesus was the first Man in history who lived perfectly as the image of God, and through His life, suffering, death, resurrection, and ascension, He began a new race[2] of human image bearers. As we have seen, He has shared His assignment with us and prayed we would function in the world the way He did.

Jesus' prayer in John 17 is a prayer for a people who will display God's image in this age.

A People in His Image

When God formed man to bear His image, He had a specific image in mind. The prophets saw repeated glimpses of this image:

---

[1] Crispin Fletcher-Louis, *Jesus Monotheism*, (Eugene: Cascade Books, 2015), 283.

[2] "New species" is a valid interpretation of "new creation." Romans 6:5; 1 Corinthians 15:20; 2 Corinthians 5:17; Philippians 3:20–21; Ephesians 2:15; 2 Thessalonians 2:14.

95 What Does God Want?

> *In the thirtieth year, in the fourth month, on the fifth day of the month, as I was among the exiles by the Chebar canal, the heavens were opened, and I saw visions of God (Ezekiel 1:1)*

> *And above the expanse over their heads there was the likeness of a throne, in appearance like sapphire; and seated above the likeness of a throne was a likeness with a human appearance. And upward from what had the appearance of his waist I saw as it were gleaming metal, like the appearance of fire enclosed all around. And downward from what had the appearance of his waist I saw as it were the appearance of fire, and there was brightness around him. . . . so was the appearance of the brightness all around. Such was the appearance of the likeness of the glory of the LORD. And when I saw it, I fell on my face, and I heard the voice of one speaking. (vv. 26–28)*

> *I saw in the night visions, and behold, with the clouds of heaven there came one like a son of man, and he came to the Ancient of Days and was presented before him. (Daniel 7:13)*

Throughout the Old Testament, the prophets repeatedly saw God in the form of a man, hinting at God's purpose,[3] and when they saw this image of God, they were usually terrified because of the majesty associated with this image of God. What the saints did not realize was that this form was not just God's form; *it was their form*. When the image the prophets saw put on real flesh in the person of Jesus, God's mystery was revealed, and Jesus opened up a path for humans to become the image God always intended—a people who are images of the form seen by the prophets.

Jesus enables us to fulfill the assignment first given to man.

The plan of redemption is a forward looking plan, not a backward looking one. Jesus did not come to restore the image of Adam. He came to enable man to become what God always wanted. God began a process with Adam, but the image of God reflected in Adam and all subsequent humans was just the beginning.

God always intended man to be shaped and formed into the image of Jesus.

---

[3]Genesis 16:7–11; 21:17; 22:11–16; 31:11; 32:24–30; Exodus 3:2; 23:21–24; Numbers 20:16; 22:22–35; Judges 2:1–4; 6:11–22; 13:3–21; Zechariah 1:11; 3:1–6; Ezekiel 1:26; Daniel 7:13.

It is easy to view the fall as an expected disruption to God's design for man and redemption as a costly plan to restore creation to the condition it had before the fall. However, this is not the message of the Bible. As perplexing as it is, the Bible tells the story of an unfolding mystery in which the rebellion of man and this entire age are part of God's design to produce what God always wanted.

God did not form creation to replicate the image of Adam. He formed creation to produce the image of His Son in a creature we call man.

As we have seen, this was at the heart of Paul's summary of the gospel in 1 Corinthians:

> *Thus it is written, "The first man Adam became a living being"; the last Adam became a life-giving spirit. . . . The first man was from the earth, a man of dust; the second man is from heaven. . . . Just as we have borne the image of the man of dust, we shall also bear the image of the man of heaven. (15:45, 47, 49)*

Adam was the first man—the beginning of something. Jesus is the last Man, the Man God was always after. God created man to bear His image, but that image was never complete in Adam. To bear God's image, we must be made like the Man from heaven. Our redemption in Jesus does not take us back to Adam; it enables us to become the humans God always wanted: creatures who are fully man and yet filled with God, creatures who are a unique union of heaven and Earth.

An ancient image (idol) of a god was not only a statue that looked like the god. It was a contact point with the god, a manifestation of the god. Man was made this way. Other than the person of Jesus, man can never be divine, but man is a living manifestation and contact point to the one, true living God. Because man is a living image and not an inert idol, the life of God must dwell in man for man to be a genuine image.

Only a God-infused human can properly image God, so God designed a plan to recreate man to enable humans to remain fully human and yet be infused with the life of God so deeply that they could not be separated from the God living inside them. God always had this "new species" of man in mind. It seems impossible, but it is made possible through Jesus' suffering, death, resurrection, ascension, and what the Holy Spirit accomplishes in the new birth.

The beauty of the gospel is that God is using the fall to accomplish what He always wanted, though we cannot fully grasp how He has done it. We can only look into the mystery with awe and participate in it.

GOD WANTS IMAGE BEARERS

God wants a people who bear His image—a people who are like Him—not just a people forgiven from sin.

Evangelism is a critical first step, but Jesus did not commission us to evangelize. He commissioned us to make disciples:

> *Go therefore and make disciples of all nations, baptizing them in the name of the Father and of the Son and of the Holy Spirit, teaching them to observe all that I have commanded you. And behold, I am with you always, to the end of the age. (Matthew 28:19–20)*

The commission to make disciples requires evangelism, but too often the task of missions is reduced to evangelism. However, God gives us free salvation so we can embrace the process of becoming like Him. God cannot have the kind of fellowship He deeply wants with a people who are forgiven yet do not share His loves, desires, joys, and pains.

We must become like God to live as His image.

If we want to give Jesus what He wants, we need to do the difficult, daily work of discipleship to see a people shaped into His image, loving what He loves and hating what He hates. As we seek to obey all His commandments, we become an accurate image of God in the world. If we receive forgiveness but do not embrace transformation, we cannot be God's image the way we were designed to be.

Do we realize that we are saying something about God in the way we live?

GOD HAS GREAT ZEAL FOR HIS IMAGE

We cannot exaggerate the Father's affection for His Son and His desire to exalt Him.[4] *Now consider the fact He has chosen to demonstrate the majesty of His Son through the church in this age.* When we take into account the zeal the Father has for His Son, this means He has far more zeal for the church than most of us can imagine.

---

[4] Psalm 2:6–9; 110; Isaiah 49:6; Matthew 3:17; Luke 9:35; Philippians 2:9–11; Hebrews 10:12–13.

The Father's zeal for a global witness of His Son and His deep desire for a people converge in the church—the people who will give the earth a witness of the Son and become the Son's eternal companion.

The Father takes deep delight in His Son, and He will give His Son the most precious reward He can give Him. The church is that reward. We frequently celebrate *our* reward of eternal life—and God wants us to—but how often do we think about our status as Jesus' reward?

When we focus on our reward of personal salvation, we emphasize evangelism over discipleship because the emphasis is human forgiveness and salvation from judgment. But if we focus on Jesus' reward in a people, we will have zeal for evangelism *and* discipleship because discipleship gives Jesus His reward in a people who have become like Him.

We are a people who are God's precious possession, and we proclaim the excellencies of Jesus as we are His shaped image:

> *But you are a chosen race, a royal priesthood, a holy nation, a people for his own possession, that you may proclaim the excellencies of him who called you out of darkness into his marvelous light. (1 Peter 2:9)*

The Father will answer Jesus' prayer. Jesus will get what He wants.

Our transformation into Jesus' image will not come from our strength, wisdom, or gifts. It will be the work of God, and a witness that Jesus is not just a unique human: *He is the Divine Human.* The mature church will not be formed from impressive humans. They are not a "better" version of humanity. Their glory, like Jesus' glory, will be found in the God who lives in them, dwells among them, and works through them.

When God has fully formed His people, we will not look at ourselves as the people of God and say, "Look at how awesome we are." Instead, we will say, "Look at how awesome He is. He took a people who are low, humble, and weak, and He transformed and exalted them." This is God's way. Jesus was lowly and yet exalted. The same will be true for His people.

GOD'S UNDENIABLE WITNESS IN THIS AGE

God has made Himself fully known in a human. This is a profound indicator of His purposes for humanity.

The Man Jesus is the supreme revelation of God.[1] There is no greater revelation of God in all creation, and God is forming a people who will be the image of that Man. Tragically, most of the church still has a lower view of the people of God than the New Testament does. This age is a stage for God to reveal Himself, and before the age can end, God will reveal Himself in His Son *and* in His Son's people. God has already revealed Himself in His Son, and He has revealed glimpses of Himself in His people, but He is not finished. He is going to answer His Son's prayer in a spectacular way.

As we have seen, the life of Jesus is a pattern for the church. For thirty years, God shaped His Son in obscurity. Jesus was largely hidden for decades until God had fully formed His Son. When God had finished His work, Jesus was presented publicly to Israel as the Father spoke over His Son:

> *This is my beloved Son, with whom I am well pleased. (Matthew 3:17)*

In the same way, God has been shaping His church for centuries. Millions have seen glimpses of the glory of God in His people, but a moment is coming when God will reveal His people just as He revealed His Son. God will put His church on display, and the glory of Jesus will be seen in a people. God will also set an end-time stage for His glory to be seen for just over three years in this people.[2] This people will be the

---

[1] 2 Corinthians 4:4; Colossians 1:15–16, 19; 2:9; Hebrews 1:3.

[2] Daniel 7:25; 9:27; 12:7; Revelation 11:2–3; 13:5.

undeniable evidence that Jesus was sent and is still alive as the Divine Human.

The mature church is one of the key end-time revelations of God. God will reveal Himself in human form again before the age ends. This time it will be a corporate people who point others to the majesty of the Divine Human.

God will not end the age until He produces the mature end-time church, and we take part in His plan by discipleship.

GOD'S EVIDENCE

Jesus said the world will know Him first and foremost through a people who become a flesh-and-blood demonstration of Him. The church is a people patterned after Jesus, an authentic demonstration of God in this age despite the limitations of our fallen bodies. When we present evidence for the identity of Jesus, we typically begin with the Bible, the historicity of the resurrection, or truth claims. These are all valid *secondary* witnesses of the person of Jesus, but they are not the ultimate, undeniable witness that He wants.

We love to prove the reality of Jesus and the resurrection, but how many times do we appeal to the biblical witness—the people of Jesus?

To some, this may sound like a devaluing of the Bible, but it is not. The Bible stands as the unparalleled record of what God has said and a unique witness to Jesus. It contains God's words, and those words have unbelievable power. The Bible is a powerful and indispensable witness of Jesus, but if we treat the Bible as the primary witness of Jesus, we lose sight of what the Bible clearly says.

The Bible is a priceless gift given to us by God to produce the witness He wants.

The Bible gives us insight into God's plans and purposes. It serves as the authoritative record of what God wants and the gauge of truth. It is a precious tool that leads us to the knowledge of God and keeps us from error. It is a divine instruction manual for the church to enable the people of God to become what God wants. Recognizing what Jesus plainly stated about His people does not devalue the Bible. On the contrary, it reveals our deep need of the Bible.

When the gravity of the assignment Jesus has given us fully sets in, we will love our Bibles more and not less.

If Jesus had asked the Father to primarily reveal Him through the Bible, we could simply point people to a book. It would not require a radical shift in our lives. The task Jesus has given us, on the other hand, requires us to turn to the Bible and allow it to deeply shape every area of our lives so we can become what Jesus commissioned us to be.

First and foremost, Jesus' task was the revelation of God, and Jesus has given that task to a people. One scholar's summary of Jesus' prayer is staggering:

> Central among the elements of promise is mission: "as thou didst send me into the world so I have sent them into the world" (17:18). . . . The implications are momentous. The role of the community is plainly the same as that of Jesus himself.[3]

Compare Jesus' words about Himself in John to His words about His people in the Sermon on the Mount:

> *Again Jesus spoke to them, saying, "I am the light of the world. Whoever follows me will not walk in darkness, but will have the light of life." (John 8:12)*

> *"You are the light of the world. A city set on a hill cannot be hidden. Nor do people light a lamp and put it under a basket, but on a stand, and it gives light to all in the house. In the same way, let your light shine before others, so that they may see your good works and give glory to your Father who is in heaven. (Matthew 5:14–16)*

Jesus is the "light of the world," yet our task as Jesus' body is so significant *we* can be referred to as the light of the world in this age. The implications of Jesus' words are staggering.

Do we embrace our own discipleship with this purpose? Do we disciple people with this in mind?

We know the weaknesses and failure of the people who make up the church, but we must ask a question: *Do we have more confidence in human weakness or in the Word of God? Do you believe Jesus' words are true and His Father fulfills every one of His requests?*

Jesus is the revelation of who God is, and the world must know Jesus to know God. Jesus intends the world to discover Him *through His*

---

[3] John Ashton, *Understanding the Fourth Gospel* (Oxford University Press: New York, 2009), 486.

people. We cannot give a witness to Jesus with words alone—it requires a people who are being conformed to His image.

When we do not fully engage in discipleship, we keep the world from the revelation of God.

This is more central to missions than we realize. When we think of reaching an unreached area with the gospel, we typically focus on Bible translation, media, and other evangelistic tools. These are all important and necessary tools, but they are only the beginning of reaching the unreached. For a people to be "reached," they need a biblical witness of the person of Jesus. That witness is a people—the church—in a place.

Unreached regions *must* have the Scriptures and other resources, but above all they need the witness of the people of God in their midst—a people who live among a people as an imperfect yet authentic image of Jesus, providing that people with undeniable evidence of the existence of Jesus. Our commitment to reaching unreached people must go beyond the initial stage of Bible translation and biblical resources. If we are committed to reaching the unreached, we must be committed to the long-term process of discipleship to see the people of Jesus established in an area. Until this people exists, a region does not have a complete witness of Jesus.

Some may say the church has not been a very good witness throughout history. There is some truth to this, but it does not change God's plan.

Jesus asked the Father to make the church an undeniable witness of His identity. We must have more confidence in Jesus' plan than what we perceive. We do not have liberty to change God's plan. Furthermore, for the last two thousand years, the true church has been a witness of Jesus. As a result, far more people have come to Jesus through personal interaction with a believer than mass evangelism.[4]

JESUS' PRIMARY WITNESS
We must agree with Jesus about His church to disciple correctly.

It is easy to see deficiencies in the church, but the Father will give Jesus everything He asks for. Any deficiencies we see in the witness of

---

[4]Gary L. McIntosh, *Evaluating the Church Growth Movement,* (Grand Rapids: Zondervan, 2004), 8.

the church should provoke us to intensify our commitment to active discipleship to see the church become what Jesus proclaimed it to be.

Does the condition of the church provoke us to accusations or action?

We have to put more confidence in what Jesus has said than what we see, feel, or think in any one moment. It was difficult to see Jesus' glory during His crucifixion, but Jesus' exaltation gives us the confidence God will do what He has said no matter how discouraging it may seem in any one moment.

Discipleship is partnering with Jesus to fulfill John 17.

Jesus was often derided as a mere human.[5] Many could not perceive His glory, and the same is true of the church. Many cannot see the glory God is forming. They mock and accuse the corporate body of Jesus. We must avoid this sin because it is another expression of mocking of Jesus in the flesh.

The Father has an incredible zeal for His Son so we can be sure the Father will give His Son a stunning witness through His people before the age ends.

---

[5]Matthew 13:46, 55–58; Mark 6:4–5; Luke 4:22–24; John 12:34.

Finishing the Task

In Matthew 24, Jesus gave the church a task that must be fulfilled before the age will end:

And this gospel of the kingdom will be proclaimed throughout the whole world as a testimony to all nations, and then the end will come. (v. 14)

There are still around two billion people who have not heard the gospel,[1] but for the first time in history it is possible for the gospel to be carried to all people within a generation, if we focus intentional effort on the task. Because it is possible to finish this incredible task within a generation, it is critical we know what the task is and what it will take to fulfill it.

Jesus said that the gospel of the kingdom must be proclaimed as a testimony, and the "gospel of the kingdom" is a very specific message. It is more than a message of individual salvation. It is the message of Jesus as the great King who will redeem the cosmos.[2] Jesus is the great King,[3] and He is the main focus of the gospel of the kingdom. When we proclaim this gospel, we proclaim *Him*.

The gospel will be proclaimed as a "testimony" to all people groups.[4] The word *testimony* (μαρτύριον) was used to refer to a legal

---

[1] Patrick Johnstone, *The Future of the Global Church* (Downers Grove: InterVarsity Press, 2014), 161.

[2] For more on the gospel of the kingdom, see the book, *Son of Man: The Gospel of Daniel 7*.

[3] Matthew 27:37; Mark 15:12, 26; Luke 23:38; John 19:15; Acts 17:7; 1 Timothy 6:15; Revelation 17:14; 19:16.

[4] "Nations" does not mean political entities. It is better defined as people groups.

witness, and the witness of the gospel can be compared to the testimony of a witness in a courtroom. With this in mind, Jesus predicted the gospel of the kingdom must be proclaimed to all people groups in such a way that it is a *legal, authoritative* witness of Jesus to all the people groups of the earth. This proclamation of the gospel will be the equivalent of an indisputable testimony given in a courtroom.

The church is Jesus' "star witness" in the courtroom of the age.

THE MESSENGER IS THE MESSAGE

There is increasing emphasis on mobilizing the church to fulfill this task and give this witness of the gospel to all people. This focus of this task usually centers on how to reach every people group and what the content of the gospel of the kingdom should be. The content of the message is very important, but it is only one component of the testimony that must be given. If the person who gives a testimony is not credible and compelling, their testimony will lack authority and impact.

The combination of a powerful message and a persuasive witness gives a testimony power.

When Jesus asked the Father to make His people the primary source of credibility for the gospel message,[5] He established the methodology for the witness that must go to all people. While every tool possible should be used to communicate the message of the gospel, Jesus asked the Father to make His people the primary witness of the gospel. We should broadcast the gospel via printed resources, satellite tv, internet, and every sort of media, but this is not enough to finish the task of witnessing the gospel.

Until an image-bearing, message-bearing people exist among all peoples of the earth, the task of Matthew 24:14 is not finished. Because we have unprecedented tools for communication, it is very important we understand what Jesus wants. He wants more than the propagation of information. He wants the message proclaimed by a people who are the living evidence of the message they carry. Mass media evangelism is important but not enough. If we want to see the task of Matthew 24:14 finished, we must wholeheartedly take up the task of discipling a people into the image of Jesus.

---

[5] John 17:21, 23.

We have given a lot of attention to the message of the gospel, but we need equal attention to the formation of the messengers who carry the message.[6]

The power of the gospel of the kingdom is conveyed in the message *and* by the messengers who speak it. If we want to mobilize missions to fulfill the task, we must disciple people into the image of Jesus so they can proclaim the testimony of Jesus the way He intends it. In our eagerness to finish the task, we can easily emphasize propagating a message and lose sight of the formation of the messengers.

If we only had Matthew 24:14, we would assume propagating the message of the gospel would fulfill the task, so Jesus gave us the Great Commission. The Great Commission is the methodology necessary to fulfill Matthew 24:14:

> *Go therefore and make disciples of all nations, baptizing them in the name of the Father and of the Son and of the Holy Spirit, teaching them to observe all that I have commanded you. And behold, I am with you always, to the end of the age. (Matthew 28:19–20)*

Notice Jesus did not say evangelize all nations. Evangelism is implied, but Jesus instructed us to give ourselves to the task of discipleship for the sake of missions. *God's primary evangelistic tool is a people who are living witnesses of His Son.* Communication of the gospel is obviously required for that witness, but it is the easiest part of the witness. Mass evangelism and mass communication of the gospel are good, but they will not complete the Matthew 24:14 task. The task of Matthew 24 can only be fulfilled by a people.

The apostle Paul understood and followed this pattern. In his letters, you find his burning zeal to see the gospel proclaimed to people who had not heard.[7] Paul, however, never gave a single instruction to go share the gospel among the unreached. This is one of the most perplexing things in Paul's letters unless you realize Paul's methodology was built on the Great Commission.

Instead of instructions to go speak to the unreached, Paul wrote letter after letter filled with instructions, rebukes, and encouragements

---

[6] Ultimately, the messengers are the entire body of Jesus.

[7] Romans 15:20.

to local churches. He sent his best associates to strengthen local churches. In short, Paul gave his strength and his energy to discipleship. He knew that, as people were transformed into the image of Jesus in the greenhouse of the church by ongoing, active, and intentional discipleship, they would become witnesses the Holy Spirit could send to the unreached.

A Witness Is More than Words

Paul mobilized missions by discipling people in the context of the church, not by recruiting people for missions. His methods must shape our missiology.

When you read Paul's letters and his work in Acts, you are reading a man laboring to fulfill Matthew 24:14. He followed Jesus' instructions, and God worked through him to transform the world.

A people must be shaped and formed into Jesus' image. They will proclaim the gospel of the kingdom as a living expression of the message they carry. This does not mean they must be perfect, strong, or even an entirely mature people. It means their life is a union of their humanity and the Spirit of God to the extent that they are an indisputable witness that Jesus lives.

We should teach people the information of the gospel, but we must remember that the messenger is also the message.

Paul is the most visible apostle in the New Testament. This does not automatically mean he is the greatest, but his life and methods were recorded for us as the pattern. Paul is more than a historical figure; he is also a prototype. He shows how the early mission of the church began *and* predicts how it must end.

The missions movement began with Paul's methodology, and the missions movement at the end of the age must return to his methodology.

Paul's letter to the Corinthians contains an example of New Testament missiology:

> *And I, when I came to you, brothers, did not come proclaiming to you the testimony of God with lofty speech or wisdom. For I decided to know nothing among you except Jesus Christ and him crucified. And I was with you in weakness and in fear and much trembling, and my speech and my message were not in plausible words of wisdom, but in demonstration of the Spirit and of power, so that your faith might not rest in the wisdom of men but in the power of God. (1 Corinthians 2:1–5)*

Notice Paul explicitly says his communication was not particularly powerful. He was not eloquent or a compelling speaker, a point Paul brought up again in his second letter to the Corinthians when he compared himself to other ministers.[8] Considering the importance of persuasive speech in Greek culture, Paul's words are especially significant. Paul's message was not found in his words, but in the demonstration of the Spirit and power. While the witness of power by the Spirit should include signs, wonders, and miracles, Paul was pointing to a different demonstration. He describes the demonstration in another letter to the Corinthians:

> *For God, who said, "Let light shine out of darkness," has shone in our hearts to give the light of the knowledge of the glory of God in the face of Jesus Christ. But we have this treasure in jars of clay, to show that the surpassing power belongs to God and not to us. We are afflicted in every way, but not crushed; perplexed, but not driven to despair; persecuted, but not forsaken; struck down, but not destroyed . . . so that the life of Jesus may also be manifested in our bodies. (2 Corinthians 4:6–10)*

God had given Paul "light of the knowledge of the glory of God in the face of Jesus," and this treasure was the "surpassing" (superior) power of God on display in Paul despite the weakness of his frame. Paul had become a witness—a living demonstration of Jesus. God's power was on display in Paul in a way that revealed the glory of Jesus. Paul certainly gave verbal witness to the gospel, but the power of his witness was not found in his words—it was found in who he was.

Paul warned that, if the power of preaching is found in eloquent wisdom, it empties the cross of its power. Jesus commissioned him to

> *preach the gospel, and not with words of eloquent wisdom, lest the cross of Christ be emptied of its power. (1 Corinthians 1:17)*

Paul warned that persuasive words could hinder the biblical witness of the gospel because the power of preaching comes from the presence of Jesus' own life in a human frame. The gospel should be preached by the witness of Jesus in a person who has been transformed by the cross. Paul was nervous—to the point of fear and trembling—that

---

[8] 2 Corinthians 11:6.

people would be more captured by his speech than the power of his life.

The Lord was so zealous for Paul, He *gave* Paul a painful experience of weakness so that Paul's great revelation would not lead him to pride and arrogance.[9] Paul pleaded with the Lord three times to deliver him, and the Lord's answer was surprising:

> *But he said to me, "My grace is sufficient for you, for my power is made perfect in weakness." (2 Corinthians 12:9)*

Jesus' dealing with Paul is not an aberration; it is an example to encourage us. Do you realize God may introduce weakness and pressure into your life for your own sake? When we are submitted to God's leadership, what the world considers "weakness" becomes a conduit for a greater experience and demonstration of the power of God.

If we seek power primarily in communication style and word choice, it empties the cross of its power.

We see this demonstrated all the time. You can hear a brilliant speaker on a topic but be completely unmoved by their presentation. Their information and skill may be impressive, but their life does not communicate anything. They may give information, but they are not a witness. Contrast that to someone who may speak plainly and be less educated but has clearly been transformed by the Spirit. These people are living witnesses. Whenever you encounter them, they immediately challenge you because they are a witness of Jesus. Whether you hear a person like this speak to a crowd or meet them over coffee, you immediately encounter something more than words—you encounter Jesus.

This kind of witness was not unique to Paul. Many of the most powerful witnesses in the Bible were not particularly eloquent. Moses was not.[10] Jeremiah did not know how to speak when he was called.[11] Peoples' response to the prophets indicates many of the prophets were

---

[9] 2 Corinthians 12:7–8.

[10] Exodus 4:10

[11] Jeremiah 1:6.

not considered impressive speakers. John the Baptist was the height of prophetic witness,[12] and when Jesus spoke about him, Jesus said "What did you go to *see*?" not "What did you go to *hear*?" John was among the greatest, and he was a witness because of what he *was*, not simply because of what he said.

God has frequently given His witness through people who lacked eloquence and who were weak in themselves. Many prophets faced discouragement, intimidation, self-doubt, despair, and even failure.[13] They were powerful witnesses because God's life worked through them. We imagine they were all powerful orators, but the Bible does not describe them this way.

The end-time witness of the church will be the most profound witness in history and will not come through eloquence or a "strong" people. It will come through a people who have embraced discipleship and become living evidence of the message they carry.

Many assume "maturity" results in prominence, fine honed gifts, and impressive human strength. On the contrary, this mindset is not biblical. It is a distortion of biblical maturity that prevents people from being fully discipled, discipling others properly, and coming into true biblical maturity.

We must abandon our fascination with being "strong" and "impressive" in order to come into maturity. If we break this fascination now, we can begin to move on into maturity, but if we do not, we will suffer loss when God confronts human strength in the days ahead and shatters it in His kindness. God has incredible zeal to bring the church to full maturity, so He will deal with our human strength.

Moses and Daniel predicted God is committed to saving Israel by breaking her confidence in her own strength.[14] His way with Israel is not an anomaly. If He is going to bring Israel to maturity this way, He will do the same for all His people.

---

[12]Matthew 11:11.

[13]For examples see 1 Kings 19:10; Jeremiah 20:7–18; Matthew 23:35; Hebrews 11:37.

[14]Deuteronomy 32:36; Leviticus 26:19; Daniel 12:7.

> *We continue to look for better ways to speak and communicate the gospel with more persuasive methods. This is a valuable but secondary work. We need to prioritize shaping people to become witnesses.*

YOU WILL BE MY WITNESSES

Before He ascended, Jesus commissioned the disciples to become witnesses:

> *But you will receive power when the Holy Spirit has come upon you, and you will be my witnesses in Jerusalem and in all Judea and Samaria, and to the end of the earth. (Acts 1:8)*

When we read this verse, we should hear Jesus saying, "I am going to give you the indwelling Spirit so you can answer My prayer to the Father and become the undeniable evidence that I am alive."

Witnesses communicate what they have seen and heard,[15] so discipleship must begin by beholding. The church is a community of people who have beheld Jesus together and become living witnesses of Him as we are transformed into His image.[16]

Discipleship is the process in which God turns a person into His letter—His message to the world.

Because of what Jesus has done, the church is now equipped to fulfill the Old Testament promise that God will write His message on human hearts instead of tablets of stone:[17]

> *For this is the covenant that I will make with the house of Israel after those days, declares the LORD: I will put my law within them, and I will write it on their hearts. And I will be their God, and they shall be my people. (Jeremiah 31:33)*

Discipleship produces people who become like Jesus and can then become His witnesses—His evidence—among all the peoples of the world. It's an ongoing labor to see John 17 fulfilled.

---

[15] Acts 22:5.

[16] For more on this, see the companion book, *Discipleship Begins with Beholding.*

[17] See also Exodus 31:18; 32:15; Ezekiel 11:19; 36:26.

When we think of the mission, we think of rapidly evangelizing people with a message, but we need to think seriously about what kind of people God wants to deliver that message. If we do not, we can think we are "speeding up" missions when in fact we are impeding it.

In our time, there is increasing zeal for reaching the unreached, and this zeal is an expression of the Lord's desire. However, this zeal must be yoked to a biblical missiology. You cannot grow the church the way you grow corporations. We must follow the apostolic path found in the New Testament. That path reveals church formation and the discipleship of the church community are more critical for reaching the unreached than mass evangelism (though obviously mass evangelism plays a part in the larger mission.).

It is time to abandon corporate methods of church expansion. The early church was established because apostolic messengers embraced this path and sowed their lives into communities. The technology we have access to is an incredible gift, but it will not replace the apostolic path. Until we recover these apostolic patterns which seem inconvenient and inefficient to our modern ways of thinking, we will not see the breakthroughs we see in local congregations *and* among the unreached.

John 17 must shape the way we do ministry.

Are you laboring in your local churches to inform people or produce witnesses?

THE REVELATION OF THE MYSTERY

In Ephesians, Paul summarized the revelation of the mystery of Jesus:

> *When you read this, you can perceive my insight into the mystery of Christ, which was not made known to the sons of men in other generations as it has now been revealed to his holy apostles and prophets by the Spirit. This mystery is that the Gentiles are fellow heirs, members of the same body, and partakers of the promise in Christ Jesus through the gospel. (3:4–6)*

If you ask believers, "What is the mystery of Christ?" you will probably get many different answers, but Paul identified the revelation of the mystery of Jesus *as a people—a new humanity*. When you study Paul's letters carefully, you find that his labor and theology focused on this revelation of Jesus in and through a new humanity. The question is where did Paul get the profound revelation that the mystery of Christ is a people?

Paul understood the revelation of the mystery of Jesus because of his insight into John 17.

The mystery of Christ will be revealed in a unified people who come from radically different backgrounds and are forged into a corporate "one new man."[1] This "mystery" is the people Jesus prayed for, and Paul's insight into the mystery in Ephesians is an exposition of Jesus' prayer.

The revelation of the mystery of who Jesus is must come through a people because this is what Jesus asked the Father for. This mystery has been revealed now because it was not possible prior to Jesus' appearing and the outpouring of the Spirit. The mystery was revealed

---

[1]Ephesians 2:14–15.

when God revealed Himself as a man in the person of Jesus, and it continues to be unveiled as God forms a new humanity—a people like Himself.

There is a corporate calling on the church to demonstrate the nature of God through a new humanity who has become like Jesus through the work of the indwelling Spirit:

> *Therefore, if anyone is in Christ, he is a new creation. The old has passed away; behold, the new has come. (2 Corinthians 5:17)*

"New creation" means "new creature" and can be translated "new species." The difference between one who is born again and one who is not is much greater than every other human distinction including nationality, ethnicity, race, or gender. If you have been born again by the Spirit, you are a new species of human. Jesus is different from every other human because He is God, and when you become a Christian, you are remade in that pattern.

When you become a new creation, you become a fusion of God and man that does not make you divine, and yet you can no longer separate your humanity from His indwelling Spirit.

Paul understood this *new humanity* is what Jesus died for. It is the answer to Jesus' prayer to the Father, and it was always God's intention.[2] This *one new man* is both Jesus' desire *and* His primary witness in this age. In order for Jesus to be fully known, there must be a corporate people who demonstrate the nature of Jesus.

Paul's deep love for Jesus compelled him to give his life to see this people formed. He did not hesitate to take any steps necessary to see this corporate people formed. This included willingly suffering in Philippi[3] and even rebuking one of Jesus' favorite disciples.[4]

Paul was willing to endure all manner of hardships compelled by love because he knew two things about the church:

---

[2] Genesis 12:3; 28:14; Deuteronomy 32:21; Psalm 22:27; Isaiah 24:14–16; 42:10–12; 49:6; 56:6–7; 60:1–3; 65:1; Jeremiah 16:19–21; Amos 9:11–12; Zechariah 2:11; 14:16; Malachi 1:11; Matthew 24:14; 28:19; Acts 1:6–8; Romans 15:9; Revelation 5:9; 7:9.

[3] Acts 16:35–39.

[4] Galatians 2:11–14.

- Jesus asked the Father for a people as the reward to His suffering—Paul took deep delight in giving his life to see Jesus receive the reward of His suffering.
- Jesus asked the Father to make His corporate people the primary and indisputable witness of Jesus in this age—Paul wanted everyone to know the revelation of Jesus, and he understood Jesus would be made known primarily through a people, so he labored tirelessly for a people who would become a witness and make Jesus known in this age. His love for Jesus drove him to see a vibrant witness emerge.

Paul understood why Jesus' last assignment to the church was not to evangelize but *disciple*. This does not minimize evangelism, because the ability to disciple someone assumes evangelism has taken place. However, evangelism is not enough to produce what Jesus wants.

Paul's personal hardships included physical suffering, prison, hunger, weariness, discouragement, and depression.[5] Additionally, he dealt with rejection, immaturity, strife, factions, and severe compromise in the churches.[6] None of this discouraged him, however, because he was compelled by love and a vision for who the church is in Jesus.

Do we share Paul's love for Jesus and his vision of the church? If we do not, we will not disciple rightly. We will get discouraged and quit, or we will settle for something that is superficial.

A CORPORATE PEOPLE

Jesus is not a polygamist. He is joined to one Bride—a corporate people. If we want to be His companion, we must become part of a people. Through Jesus' blood, we become part of the people who are joined to Him.

With this in mind, we need to reconsider Jesus' words in John 17:20–21:

> *I do not ask for these only, but also for those who will believe in me through their word, that they may all be one, just as you, Father, are in*

---

[5]Acts 16:23–24; 22:24; 24:27; 26:29; 28:17; 2 Corinthians 1:8; 4:8–12; 6:3–10; 11:23–28; Philippians 1:13; 2 Timothy 1:8; 2:9.

[6]For example, 1 Corinthians 1:12–13; 5:1; 6:1.

> me, and I in you, that they also may be in us, so that the world may believe that you have sent me.

Notice Jesus wants His people to become one so we can enter into fellowship with the Trinity. God will not let us come into this kind of intimate union with the Trinity as isolated individuals or as members of homogenous churches. If we want to fully experience life in the Trinity, we must boldly and actively pursue what Paul described as "one new man," a corporate people who come from very different backgrounds and yet are forged together as a unified people.

When we do not live together as a corporate people from different races, ethnicities, nationalities, and social statuses, we limit our experience of God. Our enemy knows this, so he encourages apathy, sows division, and stirs strife. Of all his weapons, apathy may be the most effective.

Ancient Israel is a prototype of what God wants. When God brought Israel out of Egypt, many Egyptians joined the people as a "mixed multitude." God then gathered the tribes of Israel around Mount Sinai and came down in their midst. The symbolism is clear. They were a single, united people gathered around His presence and made up of many individual tribes.

God wanted Israel to be a prototype of what would come, but throughout Israel's history the nation descended into tribalism and strife. To this day there has never been a full restoration of the "northern" and "southern" tribes of Israel that split apart nearly 3,000 years ago. However, we should be slow to critique Israel. We have been given the incredible gift of the indwelling Spirit, and yet we continue to tolerate tribalism and show little concern for true unity with others in the body of Jesus who are not like us.

Jesus wants to receive a corporate people as His reward, and He has given His glory to a corporate people.[7] Therefore, His people must not be divided along racial, social, ethnic, cultural, or economic lines. When we allow this, we deprive Jesus of His reward and His witness to this age.

The diverse church is a demonstration of the Trinity—distinct persons joined together in a single, corporate entity. The individuals within the church express their beautiful distinctions, they do not all

---

[7] John 17:22.

become the same, and yet they are one corporate people, just as the Trinity is three distinct persons and yet one God. Whenever we divide the church, it becomes an incomplete demonstration of the nature of God and an incomplete witness of Jesus because individual humans cannot reveal the mystery of Jesus. The mystery is only revealed in the corporate body.

God reveals Himself in relationship, and the same is true for His people. He is a single God, yet He exists in community with Himself in a relationship between three divine Persons that is impossible to fully comprehend. The church is a corporate people formed according to this pattern.

When we pursue individualism above the corporate body, we demonstrate that we are content with a limited revelation of who Jesus is.

A divided community where certain gifts or certain people groups are not valued cannot become the demonstration God wants. A body without a hand or a foot is incomplete, and the same is true of churches that do not embrace all the implications of the one new man.

Many believers agree with the concept of one new man but do not pursue the reality.

Using the analogy of the body,[8] every believer would agree that the church needs the "hands" and "feet" of the body attached and fully functioning. However, many believers are perfectly content to live without them. As a result, we have distorted and disfigured churches. Some churches are like bodies missing hands and feet, yet they are perfectly content. Other churches invite the hands and feet to join but do not allow them to fully function as part of the body. These churches are like a disfigured human body with a limb that is attached but unable to function.

Consider this: Paul had so much zeal for the corporate body that he once publicly rebuked one of Jesus' favorite disciples over the issue:

> *But when Cephas came to Antioch, I opposed him to his face, because he stood condemned. For before certain men came from James, he was eating with the Gentiles; but when they came he drew back and separated himself, fearing the circumcision party. And the rest of the Jews acted hypocritically along with him, so that even Barnabas was led astray by*

---

[8] 1 Corinthians 12:18–26; Colossians 1:18, 24; Ephesians 1:23; 4:15–16.

> *their hypocrisy. But when I saw that their conduct was not in step with the truth of the gospel, I said to Cephas before them all, "If you, though a Jew, live like a Gentile and not like a Jew, how can you force the Gentiles to live like Jews?" (Galatians 2:11–14)*

Imagine what this scene was like. Paul was the "least" of the apostles.[9] He had firmly rejected Jesus and persecuted the church before his conversion, while Peter was one of Jesus' inner circle—one of Jesus' favorite disciples. What did it take for Paul to publicly rebuke a man who was one of Jesus' favorites? The scene was incredibly awkward, but Paul was compelled.

Paul's rebuke of Peter demonstrates his understanding of Jesus' desire and his zeal for it.

If we read this interaction as Peter's error, we have missed the point. Paul notes that others, even Barnabas, were caught in the error. The point is clear: If one of Jesus' closest friends could get caught up in this error, then so can we. Peter's error is our error. We may speak about one new man like Paul, but in reality many of us live like Peter did in that moment.

Paul's rebuke was sharp and public because he recognized the gospel was at stake. Do we realize the gospel is at stake in the way we live as a "new humanity"?

THE ADMINISTRATION OF THE MYSTERY

The revelation of the mystery of a new humanity was much more than a theological concept to Paul. He gave his life for it:

> *For this reason I, Paul, a prisoner of Christ Jesus on behalf of you Gentiles—assuming that you have heard of the stewardship of God's grace that was given to me for you. (Ephesians 3:1–2)*

Paul was a *prisoner* of Jesus for the sake of people who were not like him. Paul was Jewish. *Very* Jewish.[10] And yet he was Jesus' prisoner for the sake of people he had previously despised. Paul understood he was owned by Jesus and had been given Jesus' grace for others' sake.

---

[9] 1 Corinthians 15:9; Ephesians 3:8; 1 Timothy 1:15.

[10] Galatians 1:13–14; Philippians 3:5–6.

The grace you have been given by God is not just for your own calling. It is for the sake of others not like you so that the mystery can be revealed.

Paul did not consider this assignment a burden. Paul took deep delight in laying down his life for the sake of a formerly hostile people because he understood what would happen:

- People groups who did not know Jesus would come to know Him—Paul *gladly* suffered so that other people groups could know Jesus because he loved Jesus deeply and he understood Jesus' desire for people who did not know Him. *Does our love for Jesus compel us to pursue others not like us?*

- Paul would discover a greater revelation of the mystery of Jesus—It is one thing to have compassion on others and want them to know the gospel, but Paul understood there were aspects of Jesus he would only discover as he became one people with Gentiles he previously despised. Paul became deep friends and "family" with people who were very different from him, in part because his life was dedicated to discovering and knowing the person of Jesus.[11] *Do we realize when we neglect the biblical new humanity we limit our own revelation of Jesus?*

- Jesus would be made known—Paul knew Jesus had committed to making Himself known through a people, and he knew that people had to be a very specific kind of people. Paul labored for this kind of people so Jesus would be made known to people *and* the spiritual powers. *Do we know how Jesus wants to be made known?*

The grace given to Paul empowered him to preach Christ *and* bring to light the "administration" of the mystery:

To me, the very least of all saints, this grace was given, to preach to the Gentiles the unfathomable riches of Christ, and to bring to light what is the administration of the mystery which for ages has been hidden in God who created all things. (Ephesians 3:8–9 NASB95)

---

[11] 1 Corinthians 2:2; Philippians 3:8–10.

The mystery is not made known simply by information. There is an administration, a plan, whereby the mystery of Jesus is made known through a people. Paul not only preached Jesus, he actively participated in the administration of the mystery.

The word *administration* conveys the idea of a plan that must be executed. As Paul established churches and discipled others, he was conscious he was not merely conveying information; he was administrating—intentionally implementing—the revelation of the mystery.

Paul did not passively hope the mystery would be revealed; he took intentional steps for it to be made known. He carefully organized churches so the mystery would be made known. This administration was so sacred to Paul that he wrote about it in several of his letters.[12]

Do we actively administrate the mystery in our churches? Do we organize our churches so that Jesus will be made known in the way He asked the Father to reveal Him?

Paul followed his description of God's desire in Colossians 1 with a summary of His commission to administrate the revelation of the knowledge of Jesus:

> *I became a minister according to the stewardship from God that was given to me for you, to make the word of God fully known, the mystery hidden for ages and generations but now revealed to his saints. To them God chose to make known how great among the Gentiles are the riches of the glory of this mystery, which is Christ in you, the hope of glory. (vv. 25–27)*

"Stewardship" is another way of translating the word for *administration* (οἰκονομία). As in Ephesians, the mystery requires administration (stewardship), and the glory of the mystery is revealed as Jesus lives in a people who come from all peoples.

Paul mentioned his stewardship again in 1 Corinthians:

> *I am still entrusted with a stewardship. . . . For though I am free from all, I have made myself a servant to all, that I might win more of them. To the Jews I became as a Jew, in order to win Jews. To those under the law I became as one under the law (though not being myself under the law) that*

---

[12]See 1 Corinthians 9:17; Colossians 1:25; 1 Timothy 1:4.

I might win those under the law. To those outside the law I became as one outside the law (not being outside the law of God but under the law of Christ) that I might win those outside the law. To the weak I became weak, that I might win the weak. I have become all things to all people, that by all means I might save some. I do it all for the sake of the gospel, that I may share with them in its blessings. (1 Corinthians 9:17, 19–23)

Once again, we find Paul administrated the mystery by actively giving his life to pursue others not like him and become family with them through Jesus. He bound his life to this pursuit.

Paul understood his apostolic commission required him to live in a very specific way so that Jesus would be made known in the way Jesus asked the Father to reveal Him. Paul's stewardship was not unique to Paul. We are *all* required to administrate this mystery and answer Jesus' prayer. Church leaders are *especially* called to administrate the mystery in the sphere of responsibility the Lord has given them.

Do our churches demonstrate we understand the responsibility to administrate the mystery?

Is this mystery a priority in the design and operation of our church communities? If it is not, the Lord will orchestrate circumstances to lead us back to the apostolic path. If you are in leadership, does this mystery have priority in your ministry? Do you speak about it? Do you disciple others so their lives reveal the mystery? If this mystery is absent from your life and ministry, you are not leading the body to full maturity.

As we administrate the mystery and orient our lives around it, Jesus is revealed in our church families and in the places where we live. If we do not actively engage in the mystery, we will lack the full revelation of Jesus. And our cities will not receive the witness Jesus wants them to see.

We are called to actively administrate the mystery, and if we do not, the Father will shift our circumstances to lead us to fully engage in the revelation of His Son through the revelation of the mystery. Let's have ears to hear and become joyful prisoners of Jesus now.

RECREATING HUMANITY

The church is not merely a gathering of saved individuals. It is a context where God is recreating humanity in Jesus. Jesus has done far more than make salvation available to individuals. He is forming a new humanity that is His single companion and yet consists of many individuals.

In the church, Jesus works to provide the answer to His own prayer in John 17.

When Paul described God's design for the church, he went all the way back to the original purpose of man:

> *For we are his workmanship, created in Christ Jesus for good works, which God prepared beforehand, that we should walk in them. (Ephesians 2:10)*

Paul's description of the church as God's work created in Jesus for good works is a reference back to Genesis 1–2 where God first made man in His image to work the earth.[1] A few verses later, Paul followed this reference with another analogy to the garden. Once we understand that analogy, it gives us much more insight into why he rebuked Peter in Antioch:

> *For he himself is our peace, who has made us both one and has broken down in his flesh the dividing wall of hostility by abolishing the law of commandments expressed in ordinances, that he might create in himself one new man in place of the two, so making peace, and might reconcile us both to God in one body through the cross, thereby killing the hostility. . . . For through him we both have access in one Spirit to the Father. (Ephesians 2:14–16, 18)*

---

[1] Genesis 1:26–28; 2:15.

Paul reminded the Ephesians they had been created in Jesus by the Spirit for good works, and in verse 15, he used the word create (κτίζω) again to expound on God's creation of a new humanity. Being born again enables us to participate in God's creation of new humanity which is a corporate life and not solely an individual one.

In verse 10, Paul summarized what Jesus has done, and in verse 15, he summarized what Jesus is doing to bring this new species of humanity to maturity. Taken together, these verses have profound implications:

- In Jesus' body the deep hostility that divided people groups has been broken. Because Jesus died to bring people together, racial and ethnic unity within the body is a *core component* of the gospel.

- Jesus endured horrific suffering so He could create one new man out of Jew and Gentile. His work of new creation creates a new humanity that is made up of humans who were previously at odds. Therefore, the work of salvation depends on the unity of the body and the reconciliation of humanity in Jesus. This corporate reconciliation is a core part of our salvation which implies Jesus' work of salvation is not completed until a diverse body that is fully reconciled and unified in Him comes to maturity.

- Jesus reconciles us to God *in one body*. The work of redemption is much more than individual salvation. To be fully reconciled to God, we must be reconciled as a new humanity that is no longer divided by the walls of hostility. We are fully reconciled to God *in one body* that is ethnically and racial diverse and yet a new kind of humanity.

In this passage, Paul repeatedly speaks of two becoming one: "He . . . has made us *both one* . . . that he might create . . . *one* new man in place of the *two* . . . and . . . reconcile us *both* to God in *one* body . . . through him we *both* have access in *one* Spirit to the Father."

The theme of two becoming one is a direct allusion back to Genesis 2:

> *Then the man said, "This at last is bone of my bones and flesh of my flesh; she shall be called Woman, because she was taken out of Man." Therefore a man shall leave his father and his mother and hold fast to his wife, and they shall become one flesh. (Genesis 2:23–24)*

Paul's language was intentional, and he expected his readers to understand what God is doing in the new creation by comparing it to God's original act of creation. To understand why Paul used this analogy, we have to know how man and woman are introduced in Genesis.

GOD CREATED MAN

The word *adam* (אָדָם) can be used multiple ways in Hebrew. Its first meaning is "mankind" or "humanity," which obviously includes both male and female. When the definite article is added it becomes "the adam" and can refer to a specific human. Finally, it can be used as a name, which is the way we typically think of Adam in English. Genesis 1–3 uses the word *adam* repeatedly, and in English it is translated as man, mankind, the man, or Adam depending on context. By looking at a few examples of how adam is used, we can discover what Paul was trying to communicate in Ephesians.

In Genesis 1, God created man:

> *Then God said, "Let us make man [adam] in our image, after our likeness. And let them have dominion over the fish of the sea and over the birds of the heavens and over the livestock and over all the earth and over every creeping thing that creeps on the earth." So God created man [the adam] in his own image, in the image of God he created him; male and female he created them. (Genesis 1:26–27)*

God used plural language to refer to His creation of mankind by saying let *us* make man, which is singular, in *our* image. Then He also used plural language to refer to man by saying let *them* have dominion. At this point in Genesis, man is a singular creature, but God is already referring to man as a plural entity. This is emphasized again in the summary of man's creation in verse 27. It tells us God made *the adam* which is singular and has a definite article in Hebrew in His image and then adds that this adam was made both male and female. So this singular human is also plural, and this is part of what it means to be made in God's image.

From the very beginning, man is introduced as a single creation made in God's image, and in that image, there is more than one expression of man.

In Genesis 2, we read about "the adam" who is perfect and yet incomplete and "alone."[2] So God took "the adam" and divided him into two persons, male and female, who both come from this single adam. And when the male adam sees the female adam, he uses two new words: *Ish* (אִישׁ) which means male and *Isha* which means female. The words are used very intentionally in Genesis 2:

> *Then the man [the adam] said, "This at last is bone of my bones and flesh of my flesh; she shall be called Woman [isha], because she was taken out of Man[ish]." Therefore a man [ish] shall leave his father and his mother and hold fast to his wife, and they shall become one flesh. (Genesis 2:23–24)*

In light of what has already been said about man, the introduction of these two new words is significant. When the one man is split into two persons, the author of Genesis refers to the two expression of man using new words: *ish* (male) and *isa* (female). Then the author says the male (*ish*) should be joined to the female so they can become one flesh.

Now this may seem very technical, so let's take a moment and summarize the progression of man's creation because it is filled with meaning:

- God created a man as a single creature in the image of God. Though man was a single creature, he was intended to have a plural expression.
- The single man was perfect, but alone and not a full expression of God's image. To be a full expression, man needed to exist in community with different expressions of man.
- God divided man into two expressions: male and female. The two *together* were the complete image of God.
- When God divided man into two, the two were intended to come together and become *one flesh*. In this union, the two

---

[2]Genesis 2:18.

expressions remain, but they are reunited so that man becomes "one" again.

- When the two distinct expressions are formed together in a way that retains their distinction but formed them again into a single "adam," the creation of man is complete.

If we put all this together, we could say it this way: The image of God is reflected in one, single creature who must exist in community and have more than one expression, but these expressions must come together so deeply they become one flesh. As they do, we see a mystery: a single creature that exists in multiple expressions who is yet one being. In other words, an expression of the Trinity, a single God who exists in community as multiple persons but deeply united into one.

MARRIAGE AND THE CHURCH

Paul used Genesis because his main point was: *The church is the context where God is recreating man in Jesus into God's image.* And as mankind is recreated, Jesus' prayer will be answered.

When Paul needed an analogy to describe God's intention for the church, he used the creation story because in Jesus God is creating mankind again and because the creation story demonstrates the mystery of two becoming one. Marriage is typically considered an analogy for the relationship between God and His people. That is the ultimate meaning of marriage,[3] but Paul also used marriage as an analogy for how God's people should be joined together.

Paul saw marriage as the best analogy to describe the reconciliation of the races in Jesus, the way we should live together, and the way we should pursue each other. Do we see the church this way?

God is fully committed to reconciling *one people* to Himself who are made up of all people groups. Obviously, this means the body of Jesus is made up of far more than two ethnic groups. We are not simply "Jew and Gentile." There are thousands of gentile people groups who must also be reconciled together. However, in the context of the biblical covenants, Jew and Gentile was the great divide, and Paul used that

---

[3]Ephesians 5:32.

divide to describe God's plan and compare it to the mystery of marriage.

If we think Paul was only referring to "Jew and Gentile," we will miss Paul's message. If Jesus has resolved the biggest barrier among mankind, then barriers between Gentile and Gentile should no longer exist. If we remain isolated, separated, or detached as Gentile and Gentile, it is evidence we are not really participating in the reconciliation of Jew and Gentile. Many Gentiles speak about God's desire to reconcile Jew and Gentile, but if we are not actively reconciling with other Gentiles, we are not really pursuing reconciliation as Jew and Gentile.

Paul would be shocked to discover that, while we advocate for marriage and work hard to prevent divorce in our individual marriages, we seem very content for the body of Jesus to exist in a divorced state. Do we carry Paul's urgency for the "two" to be made "one flesh."

Moreover, Jesus is reconciling us to the Father *as one*. As we saw in John 17, there are aspects of our salvation and communion with the Trinity we only experience when we are *one flesh* in the church. If we are content with individual salvation or with the salvation of our own people group, we are satisfied with an incomplete reconciliation to God. *All people groups*[4] must be reconciled to each other in Jesus for the church to be fully reconciled to God. Our salvation must be worked out within the "household of God:"

> *So then you are no longer strangers and aliens, but you are fellow citizens with the saints and members of the household of God. (Ephesians 2:19)*

When we think of the work of salvation and the different ethnicities in the body of Jesus, do we pursue a relationship with them that could be compared to marriage? That is the analogy Paul used. We should seek to become forged together as one people with mutual concerns, interdependence, shared resources, and unified goals. The Spirit will give wisdom how to work this out in individual congregations, but it *must* become priority because it is central to the gospel and it is a priority to God.

---

[4]Matthew 24:14; Revelation 5:9; 7:9.

Are we content with a "divorced" church body that "lives" very separately with little more than a distant relationship or a few interactions a year?

Jesus broke down the wall of hostility between people groups in His own flesh. How is it that we seem relatively content to leave the barriers in place that Jesus demolished?

The Bible boldly predicts that *all* people groups must saved as one body because God wants all humanity reconciled to Him. He does not want only men, women, Jew, Gentiles, Greeks, or any other distinguishing group. He paid an awful price in His own flesh so that *all* could be reconciled together as *one*.

If we do not have this vision, we are like people content for one part of the body to be saved and the rest lost. To use the creation story, it could be compared to one half of the human, male or female, being saved and the other lost. That is not the gospel. God does not want to save men, but not women. The gospel is all human expressions saved together as one. God's glory is at stake in saving every expression of humanity and making the many one, and the age will not end until He has done it. He will have a remnant from "every tribe and tongue" because He will save *every* expression of humanity to create the one humanity He wants.

Jesus had the creation story in mind when He asked the Father for a people who are one and brought into fellowship with the Trinity. Paul's letter to the Ephesians gives us a glimpse at *what* God is doing and *how* He is doing it. Until it has come, the Bride is not mature and not ready for the return of the Bridegroom.

Jesus has waited thousands of years, but it is time for the many to become one flesh.

INSTRUCTING THE POWERS

We do not realize just how much is at stake in the makeup of the church, but the spiritual powers do. They release accusations, stir up division, promote compromise, and fuel strife in the church and the nations to wage war against the witness of Jesus. Tragically, the church often fails to resist their attacks and, at times, even cooperates with them. As long as we do not proactively address issues like racial division, social prejudices, and nationalism *in the church*, we continue to play into the hands of the powers.

A corporate people who are distinct and yet unified seems impossible because it is impossible by human means, but Jesus gets everything He prays for.

Jesus asked the Father to make His people a witness to the world (systems of this age), and the world as a system is much bigger than its human aspects. Part of the system of this world is the influence of the spiritual powers who rule in this age.[1] As Paul expounded on the "mystery" Jesus prayed for, he added a profound insight about God's plan:

> *To me, though I am the very least of all the saints, this grace was given, to preach to the Gentiles the unsearchable riches of Christ, and to bring to light for everyone what is the plan of the mystery hidden for ages in God, who created all things, so that through the church the manifold wisdom of God might now be made known to the rulers and authorities in the heavenly places. (Ephesians 3:8–10)*

Paul openly proclaimed the plan of the mystery that had been hidden. This "plan" is the unfolding of Jesus' prayer in John 17. The revelation of the plan of the hidden mystery is going to make God's manifold

---

[1] Romans 8:38; Ephesians 1:21; 2:2, 15; 3:10; 6:12; Colossians 1:16; 1 Peter 3:22.

wisdom known. What is this wisdom? As we saw in Colossians 1, Paul summarized the wisdom of God with two main themes:

1. Everything in this age exists to reveal God, and Jesus is the pinnacle of the revelation of God in the created realm.
2. This age is a context designed by God to form and shape a people into His image. It will produce a mature body that resembles the Head.

With that in mind, Paul's next statement is the logical conclusion: "through the church the manifold wisdom of God might now be made known." When we read this statement in light of John 17, Colossians 1, and many other passages, we see that God is revealing His wisdom through a people, and that wisdom revolves around God's revelation of Himself in a person *and* a corporate people.

It would be reasonable for Paul to say God's wisdom is made known through Jesus or the Scripture, but Paul explicitly says God's wisdom is being made known *through the church*. Do we have this view of the church? We might expect Paul to say the church makes God's wisdom known to people or even to the physical realm, but what Paul says next is stunning: The church is going to make God's wisdom "known to the rulers and authority in the heavenly places."

God's wisdom will be made fully known to the powers through the people Jesus prayed for.

Do we really, I mean really, grasp that the church instructs the powers in the wisdom of God as she becomes the corporate witness of Jesus in this age? Our audience is not always who we think it is. So often we focus nearly entirely on human audiences. We are encouraged (or discouraged) by how many people we see attending meetings or responding to our witness. But do we grasp we are instructing the powers in the wisdom of God?

Everything the church does is designed to instruct the powers. Your secret life when you are alone. Small gatherings of the saints for prayer, Bible study, or fellowship. Large gatherings. Secret meetings and open celebrations. Every time the church gathers, we speak to the rulers in heavenly places. The question is *what are we saying to them?*

Too many people are hoping they are well-known among people when they should ask, "Does my life reveal the wisdom of God to the rulers and authorities?"

Think about this carefully: God is instructing the powers of this age through His people. The powers are not instructed by speaking to them or rebuking them. It is not accomplished with pride, bravado, or human strength. The powers are instructed when we live our lives as a corporate demonstration of Jesus according to the revealed mystery.

Through the mystery of God's eternal purpose in Jesus and His crucifixion, people who are born enemies of God subject to the spiritual powers can become like God and instruct the powers in God's wisdom.

The wisdom of God is displayed through the power of God, so the powers are not instructed by our strength, but by our obedience and our willingness to allow God to form us. Jesus triumphed over the powers by obedience unto death, and we will triumph in a similar way. The church who instructs the powers will bear a resemblance to the crucified King who triumphed over the powers.

God is going to instruct the powers through the church *before* the return of Jesus. When Jesus returns, He will execute God's judgment,[2] and the powers will no longer rule in heavenly places. The wisdom of God will be openly manifested when Jesus returns and removes the powers' present authority. God is going to reveal His wisdom to the powers through His church *before* the church receives their resurrected bodies in the age to come.

Does your life instruct the powers?

Furthermore, are you discipling others so their lives will instruct the powers?

Everything the powers do is designed to keep this people from emerging because, when God brings this people to maturity, the powers' time is finished. As a result, the powers stir up division by accusations.[3] They stir up racial and ethnic hostility.[4] Paul understood this, so he stood strongly against factions and division in the church.[5]

---

[2]Matthew 10:15, 32; 11:22, 24; 12:27, 36, 41, 42; 13:41; 16:27; 19:28; 25:31–32; Mark 8:38; Luke 9:26; 10:14; 11:31–32; 12:8–9; 18:8; 21:36; John 3:18–19; 5:22, 24, 27, 29–30; 8:16; 9:39; 12:31, 48; 16:8, 11.

[3]Their leader is referred to as the "accuser of the brethren," so they are accusers as well. See Revelation 12:10.

[4]Matthew 24:7; 1 Corinthians 3:3. Note that "nation" is *ethnos*, which are people groups, not political nations.

[5]1 Corinthians 1:12–13; Galatians 2:11–14.

As long as the church is divided, we cannot fulfill Jesus' deep desire for a people who bear witness to Him, and whenever you see racial conflict, the powers are deeply connected to it.

As along as we are content with "disfigured" churches that do not pursue the vision of a new humanity forged from various races, ethnicities, genders, social status, and nationalities, we either do not understand the wisdom of God, or we simply do not care. And the rulers rejoice because they are not instructed or challenged.

The powers know this humanity must emerge before the return of Jesus, and they know they will not be judged until Jesus returns. Therefore, the powers are quite content for us to hold church and teach the Bible as long as we do not aggressively pursue the new humanity that Jesus asked the Father for. We tend to think the powers are motivated mainly by the desire to prevent people from escaping hell, but this is not true. They are motivated by the desire to retain their freedom and their power. They do not mind a few people embracing the gospel and even living consecrated lives as long as this does not threaten their place in the heavens. In fact, the powers are quite confident as long as we cooperate in their schemes to bring accusations and divisions.

The powers will have their confidence disrupted when the mature, unified people of God begin to emerge because they know when Jesus' prayer is answered their judgment is imminent.

People typically pursue superficial solutions to racial, ethnic, and national conflict because it's easier. Different people groups retreat to their own churches and bless each other from afar. *Beloved, this does not threaten the powers because it does not answer Jesus' prayer.* We are not called to superficial solutions, which leave the powers enthroned. We are called to difficult challenges yet rewarding solutions that will require much of us, but in the end will demonstrate the wisdom of God, threaten the powers, and ultimately answer Jesus' prayer.[6]

The rulers are willing to endure perfectly ordered, even "anointed," church services with one ethnicity over here, another over there, one nationality separated from the other, and the rich in one kind of church and poor in another. These kinds of churches may lead many to

---

[6] An excellent resource on the challenge of unity in the church is *More Than Equals* by Spencer Perkins and Chris Rice.

salvation, but they do not threaten the powers because they do not answer Jesus' prayer.

Are we willing to consider that segregated churches are an expression of the work of the spiritual powers we are called to instruct?

While the powers stir up all sorts of conflict and strife, perhaps their greatest weapon is ambivalence. The powers are even willing for us to say the right things and value unity and the mature body because many people assume saying something is the same as living it out. The truth is the powers will tolerate almost anything as long as it does not produce the kind of action that instructs them and threatens their present position.

As long as we limit the gospel to the forgiveness of sins and a heavenly retirement, the powers are not instructed and feel quite safe. We know what we have been saved *from*, but do we know what we have been saved *for*? You were not saved merely to escape hell. You were saved to answer the deepest longing of Jesus' heart and instruct the powers.

Discipleship must be designed to produce Ephesians 3:10.

OVERCOMING THE POWERS

As we saw a few chapters back, Jesus asked the Father to reveal Him to the world through His people in an undeniable way:

> *I in them and you in me, that they may become perfectly one, so that the world may know that you sent me and loved them even as you loved me. (John 17:23)*

"The world" is the system of this age that is estranged from God, and the spiritual powers are a key part of the system. Satan is the ruler of "the world"[7] and the system of this age reflects his influence and the influence of the powers. Therefore, when Jesus asked the Father to reveal Him to the world through a people, He also asked the Father to instruct the powers of this age through this people.

Paul wrote Ephesians 3:10 because of his grasp of John 17:23 and his certainty that the Father would answer Jesus' request.

---

[7] John 12:31; 14:30; 16:11; 2 Corinthians 4:4; Ephesians 2:2.

Based on John 17, Paul understood that Jesus triumphed over the powers,[8] and His people must also. Paul referred to the spiritual "powers" that resist the revelation of the knowledge of Jesus four times in Ephesians.[9] Those four verses help summarize Paul's exposition of John 17:23.

Paul referenced the powers first in Ephesians 1:

he raised him from the dead and seated him at his right hand in the heavenly places, far above all rule and authority and power and dominion, and above every name that is named, not only in this age but also in the one to come. (vv. 20–21)

Jesus has been exalted "far above" all the powers. He is the Exalted One and the revelation of God who has triumphed over the powers. The first chapter of Ephesians focuses on the supremacy of Jesus, the revelation of Jesus, and who we are in Him.

The next reference is found in Ephesians 2:

And you were dead in the trespasses and sins in which you once walked, following the course of this world, following the prince of the power of the air, the spirit that is now at work in the sons of disobedience. (vv. 1–2)

Paul's point in chapter two is straightforward: We are born "dead" in our sins and follow the course of this world, which means we follow the leadership of the prince of the powers. Without Jesus, we do not instruct the powers; we are dominated by them and live according to their wisdom. This reality set the stage for Paul's next reference to the powers in Ephesians 3:

So that through the church the manifold wisdom of God might now be made known to the rulers and authorities in the heavenly places. (v. 10)

We are born under the influence and control of the powers, but in Jesus we are so transformed that, instead of being dominated by the powers, we are called to instruct them and reveal Jesus to them. How do we do this? Ephesians 2–3 summarizes God's strategy. When we

---

[8]Colossians 2:15.

[9]Ephesians 1:21, 2:2; 3:10; 6:12

live as a "new species" and a "new (corporate) human," we instruct the powers and answer Jesus' prayer.

When we live as a new humanity, it is proof we are no longer under the influence of the powers. Conversely, if we are not actively living together as a new humanity, it reveals we remain under the influence of the powers described in Ephesians 2:1–2. Tragically, it is possible for a church to remain under the influence of the powers.

Paul's final reference to the powers is found in the last chapter in Ephesians:

> *For we do not wrestle against flesh and blood, but against the rulers, against the authorities, against the cosmic powers over this present darkness, against the spiritual forces of evil in the heavenly places. (Ephesians 6:12)*

Paul reminded the Ephesians to utilize the "armor of God" that empowers us to resist and overcome the spiritual powers who are making war against the revelation of the mystery.[10] This armor is available to enable us to instruct the powers and reveal the mystery of Jesus by living as a new humanity.

Paul commanded us to be strong and put on God's armor so we could fulfill Jesus' prayer, reveal the mystery, and instruct the powers.

Are you "putting on" this armor so you can instruct the powers by living with other believers as a new species of humanity in the context of the church? Are you discipling others to actively fight the enemy on this battlefield?

---

[10]Ephesians 6:10–11.

FUEL FOR APOSTOLIC LABOR

Jesus' prayer in John 17 fueled apostolic missions.

John 17 is the longest recorded prayer we have from Jesus, and the apostles treasured these sacred words. The disciples heard the emotion in Jesus' voice as He asked the Father for His reward. They also knew the suffering Jesus endured to secure that reward. Because they knew Jesus' desire and His suffering, the apostles gave their lives to partner with the Spirit for Jesus to receive His reward.

When you read the apostles' letters and look at their lives, you can see John 17 shaped their lives. It was a paradigm they lived by. It influenced their decisions and how they spent their lives. Because Jesus had asked the Father for a people, their primary work was to cooperate with the Holy Spirit to see this people formed.

We readily say that the "nations"[1] are Jesus reward, but "the nations" is a bit abstract. Yes, Jesus will inherit the nations, but what that really means is He wants a *people*—real humans who have cooperated with His Spirit, been formed into His image, and then forged into a corporate body.

When this people are prepared for Jesus, the age will end. It will be over because Jesus' reward will be ready.

This fueled apostolic hope and propelled apostolic labor. It enabled the apostles to be deeply involved in the mess of daily life and disciple the Gentiles. Paul endured the Corinthians when some were engaged in immorality, others were using spiritual gifts in pride to exalt themselves, and the church split according to their favorite apostles. Paul stuck with them through their immaturity because he knew Jesus

---

[1] Again, the English word *nations* in the New Testament is a translation of *ethnos* (ἔθνος), which means "people group," not political state.

wanted a people and he knew Jesus would get what He wanted so his labor was not hopeless.

So many of us want to know, "What can I do for God? How can I please Him?" We should seek the Lord to see if He has a specific assignment for us, but He has already told us what He wants:

- He wants to be known. Everything in the created realm exists so He can reveal who He is. Spend your life on an epic pursuit to know Him as He has revealed Himself in creation in the person of Jesus. Become a student of His beauty as it is revealed in Him.

- He wants a people. Disciple people and deeply join your life to His people so He gets His reward.

The Holy Spirit works *powerfully*[2] within His people to bring about the prayer of Jesus. He takes great delight in answering Jesus' prayer, and He will give us tremendous strength and might to see it come to pass. If we line up our lives with Jesus' desire, the Father will give us His own power in order to bring about what Jesus wants.

About two thousand years ago, God was killed in the most brutal way. Just before His suffering began, He made a deal: "If I am going to endure suffering, this is what I want. Give Me a people." *We cannot overestimate the Father's desire to reward Jesus for His suffering.*

When we consider Jesus' desire for a people who will suddenly come to maturity at the end of the age, it is clearly the second most important end-time theme. The only theme that is more important is the revelation of Jesus Himself. The question is do we value this end-time theme as much as Jesus does?

FAITH IN WHAT IS NOT YET SEEN

The apostles were compelled by Jesus' desire for a people, and it caused them to disciple others. The apostles discipled and endured with faith in something they had not yet seen: *a mature church.*

> *Now faith is the assurance of things hoped for, the conviction of things not seen. (Hebrews 11:1)*

---

[2] 2 Corinthians 12:9–10; 13:3; Colossians 1:29.

During Jesus' ministry before He died, it was obvious He was unlike any other human, but His glory was also veiled. Glimpses of it could be seen, but His glory was not fully revealed until the time of His suffering. Jesus' suffering radically transformed His body. His glory was suddenly manifested and seen. Who He was became visible in a way it had not been before.

The same will be true with the church.

Everyone who is born again gives glimpses of the glory of God working on their inner man, and yet there is a hidden glory not yet seen. As the age heads toward a time of final tribulation, God is going to reveal the true nature of the redeemed, and that revelation will be stunning.

Once we discover what God says about the future of His people in the pages of Scripture, we can disciple with faith. Faith is having more confidence in Bible verses than what we can see. When we live this way, we begin to live in the reality of the things those verses speak about.

The Father is fully committed to answering this prayer. Nothing can stop Him. He will not hesitate to do anything necessary to produce this people. The Father is fully committed to this because He loves His Son. As people who have been redeemed by the Son's immense suffering, how much more should we share the Father's passion to reward His Son?

The question we have to ask is what captures us more: our personal fulfillment or His reward?

We cannot let the gospel be limited to the hope of being saved from hell. When we do, we tend to focus almost entirely on evangelism. Evangelism is extremely important, but it is not the task Jesus gave us. Jesus commanded us to *disciple*. Discipleship requires evangelism as a first step, so evangelism is important. It is part of the process. However, the goal is not evangelism. The goal is discipleship —a people made like Jesus.

If evangelism were the goal, Paul and the other apostles would have done mass evangelism and moved on. Instead, they built deep relationships with people who were very different from themselves and labored with them for decades to see Jesus formed in them.[3] They

---

[3] 2 Corinthians 12:15; Philippians 2:17, 20; Colossians 1:28–29; 1 Thessalonians 2:8; 1 John 3:16.

knew the gospel is not merely a way to escape hell. The gospel is an invitation to become like God and become His companion.

The apostles' focus is abundantly clear in the apostolic prayers in the New Testament.[4] When you study their prayers carefully, you begin to notice they are all prayers for the church. They are almost exclusively "positive" prayers, which means they are prayers asking God to do something positive in His people, not prayers focused on "rebuking" things. They repeatedly prayed for God to mature a people because they were driven by Jesus' longing for a people.

---

[4]Romans 15:5–6, 13; 1 Corinthians 1:5–8; Ephesians 1:17–19; 3:16–19; Philippians 1:9–11; Colossians 1:9–11; 1 Thessalonians 3:10–13; 2 Thessalonians 1:11–12; 3:1–5.

The Most Neglected End-Time Theme

A Bride like Her Groom

Some people do not study the "end times" because the subject has been occasionally studied or applied in an unhealthy way. However, you cannot build anything properly unless you know what you are trying to build, and the same is true for discipleship. God wants us to know the end of His plan in this age so we know what kind of people He is going to produce before the age ends.

If you study the New Testament carefully, you find the main themes of Jesus' return undergirded the apostles' paradigm of the discipleship. Like them, we *must* understand the main themes of the end times and know where God is leading history to disciple people correctly.

When John encountered Jesus' glory in His exaltation, he saw something astonishing:

> *And between the throne and the four living creatures and among the elders I saw a Lamb standing, as though it had been slain. . . . (Revelation 5:6)*

The book of Revelation begins with the beauty of Jesus, but it ends with the beauty of God *and* His companion:

> *"Let us rejoice and exult and give him the glory, for the marriage of the Lamb has come, and his Bride has made herself ready; it was granted her to clothe herself with fine linen, bright and pure"—for the fine linen is the righteous deeds of the saints. (Revelation 19:7–8)*

This companion will have a body like Jesus, share His glory, and be like Him:

> *But our citizenship is in heaven, and from it we await a Savior, the Lord Jesus Christ, who will transform our lowly body to be like his glorious*

> *body, by the power that enables him even to subject all things to himself. (Philippians 3:20–21)*
>
> *To this he called you through our gospel, so that you may obtain the glory of our Lord Jesus Christ. (2 Thessalonians 2:14)*
>
> *Beloved, we are God's children now, and what we will be has not yet appeared; but we know that when he appears we shall be like him, because we shall see him as he is. (1 John 3:2)*

John saw heaven captivated by a specific demonstration of His beauty: *a Lamb who appears to be slain*. This was the highest vision of Jesus' glory John saw, indicating this is a defining characteristic of Jesus' majesty.

If Jesus appears as a slain lamb in His exalted glory, and His Bride is going to share His body and His glory, then the mature church is going to also appear as a "lamb who has been slain."

God really is a slain lamb forever. His body is permanently scarred. And He is looking for a people who resemble Him.

Jesus the Prototype

Jesus' suffering was completely unique because He is the only one whose death atoned for sin.[1] Jesus suffered for us to secure something we could not secure on our own. However, His suffering was more than a unique event. It was also a prophetic prototype of what is to come.

Jesus' life was a symbolic and unique representation of the story of Israel. Here are a few examples of this:

- When Jesus was born, a wicked king executed the babies where Jesus was born just as Pharaoh commanded the death of Israelite babies.
- Jesus came out of Egypt into the land just as Israel left Egypt in the Exodus.
- Jesus was tested in the wilderness for forty days just as Israel was tested in the wilderness for forty years.
- Jesus chose twelve disciples just as Israel had twelve tribes.

---

[1] Hebrews 9:13, 14; 10:14; 13:12.

Throughout His life, Jesus lived Israel's story, successfully overcoming where Israel had failed. Jesus not only lived Israel story throughout His life, He lived Israel's story in His death and resurrection. The Bible predicts the age will end with a time of intense suffering that lasts approximately three and a half years. At the end of the that time of suffering, God's people will be suddenly resurrected to share His glory.

Jesus' death is a prototype of end-time suffering:

- Jesus was dead for approximately three and a half days, and the end-time crisis is approximately three and a half years.

- Jesus, as the perfect Israelite, was executed by the Gentiles. Israel will come under siege by hostile gentile nations in the end-time crisis.

- Jesus was disfigured more than any other human,[2] and the end-time crisis will be a time unlike any other time.[3]

- Jesus' suffering ended with His resurrection, and the end-time crisis will end with the resurrection of God's people.[4]

For example, when Paul described Jesus' suffering as the wisdom of God,[5] he referenced Isaiah 29 which tells a story about Israel being surrounded by hostile gentile armies, going down to "death," and then being suddenly raised in glory. Paul referenced Isaiah to point out Jesus' suffering was not a strange event. Jesus was living out what Isaiah had prophesied about Israel. Some people assume this means Jesus "figuratively" fulfilled prophecies like Isaiah 29, but Paul and the apostles never said this.

Jesus clearly lived out Israel's story; however, this does not mean Israel will not also live out what the prophets predicted. Jesus was a faithful Israelite living out the

---

[2] Isaiah 52:14.

[3] Jeremiah 30:7; Daniel 12:1; Joel 2:2; Matthew 24:21.

[4] Daniel 12:1–2; 1 Corinthians 15:20–23; 1 Thessalonians 4:13–17; Revelation 20:4.

[5] 1 Corinthians 1:18–24.

end-time crisis ahead of time to give His people the confidence and courage necessary to endure their own end-time crisis.

Jesus' suffering was a prototype of the end-time crisis, and He emphasizes this with His own teaching. For example, when Jesus predicted His own suffering, He did not typically use the passages we would expect like Isaiah 53 or Psalm 22. Instead of using passages that uniquely applied to Him, Jesus preferred quoting passages like Daniel 7:25:[6]

> *He shall speak words against the Most High, and shall wear out the saints of the Most High, and shall think to change the times and the law; and they shall be given into his hand for a time, times, and half a time. (Daniel 7:25)*

> *The Son of Man is going to be delivered into the hands of men, and they will kill him. And when he is killed, after three days he will rise. (Mark 9:31)*

Jesus used the word *paradídōmi* (παραδίδωμι) for "delivered," which is the same word used for "given into" in the Greek translation of Daniel,[7] and the reference is obvious. Daniel clearly predicted the suffering of the saints, but Jesus took that prediction and applied it to Himself, making a profound statement: In His suffering, Jesus was not only securing atonement, He was also enduring the suffering of the saints. We celebrate what Jesus did for us, but we cannot overlook the fact He is the firstborn, the pattern, and the prototype. He emphasized this by applying Daniel's predictions about the saints to Himself.

Jesus' suffering was a prototype—a foreshadowing of the suffering of His people predicted by the prophets.

Until Jesus came, commentators assumed the "sufferings of Messiah" were actually the sufferings of His people and not Messiah's own personal sufferings:

> Jews of the NT era believed that the triumphal messianic age would be preceded by "woes" or sufferings. The "sufferings of Christ," therefore, "are not sufferings personally borne by the

---

[6] See also Matthew 17:22; 20:18–19; Mark 10:33–34; Luke 24:7.

[7] LXX.

Messiah . . . but sufferings associated with him, 'messianic sufferings' ushering in the messianic age in a period of woe preceding eternal bliss."[8]

Paul described Jesus as the "firstborn" of the saints, and Jesus walked through a prototype of the coming end-time tribulation that His people will walk through. Therefore, when we look at Jesus' suffering, we are seeing a prophetic foreshadowing of what His people will endure at the end of the age.

Jesus not only suffered in our place, He also endured a great tribulation of His own that foreshadows the coming great tribulation.

Jesus has shared in our suffering and walked our path, but we must still pass through our suffering and walk the path the prophets have predicted. Therefore, we must learn to read the story of Jesus in His suffering as a prototype of our suffering. He has overcome to give us courage we can overcome through His Spirit, and in His suffering we find the path we are asked to embrace.

Jesus understood that His suffering was prototypical, so He asked His followers to take up their own cross and follow Him:[9]

> *Then Jesus told his disciples, "If anyone would come after me, let him deny himself and take up his cross and follow me." (Matthew 16:24)*

We will share in His glory, but we must also walk His path. The glorious Slain Lamb will have a glorious companion who will stand alongside Him. She also will appear as a lamb slain.

With this in mind, we need to recognize Jesus' death was a prophetic event—a foreshadowing of a future time when His corporate Bride will walk the same path He walked. We must understand that path because, just as Jesus' suffering exalted Him to glory, the church's end-time suffering will also exalt her to glory alongside the Lamb.

---

[8] Paul Barnett, *The Second Epistle to the Corinthians*, The New International Commentary on the New Testament (Grand Rapids, MI: Wm. B. Eerdmans Publishing Co., 1997), 61–62, 74.

[9] See also Matthew 10:38; Mark 8:34; Luke 9:23–27; 14:27.

God designed His plan for Jesus' suffering, execution, and exaltation before history began.[10] If God planned His Son's suffering from the beginning, then God also designed a plan for Jesus' people to pass through their own suffering to produce their own exaltation and bring about the salvation of Israel. The end of the age is not simply a moment in time when the antichrist goes wild and does whatever he wishes. The Father has premeditated what is coming. He will judge all evil, but that end-time crisis will produce what He wants just as Jesus' suffering produced what He wanted.

We tend to be comfortable with the fact that the cross was God's idea, but do we realize the great tribulation is His idea as well? This thought is overwhelming, but it raises a question we must confront: Do we know God like this? Have we faced the measure to which the cross reveals who God is? If God led His Son to His own execution, He will also lead His people in ways that may shock and surprise us.

The apostles boldly declared Jesus' suffering was a horrible sin and yet also the very thing the Father desired:

> *But you denied the Holy and Righteous One, and asked for a murderer to be granted to you, and you killed the Author of life, whom God raised from the dead. To this we are witnesses. . . . "And now, brothers, I know that you acted in ignorance, as did also your rulers. But what God foretold by the mouth of all the prophets, that his Christ would suffer, he thus fulfilled." (Acts 3:14–15, 17–18)*

This same principle applies for the church. It pleased the Father to crush His Son,[11] and it also pleases Him to lead history toward the coming "great tribulation." God did not protect Jesus from His suffering. He handed Jesus over to evil men, and He predicted we will be handed over as well. That does not mean we should seek or pursue suffering, but it does mean we need to know God as He actually is and not as we have imagined Him to be.

Can we trust a God who has designed the great tribulation and will hand us over to His enemy to produce something that cannot come any other way?

---

[10] Ephesians 1:3–4; Titus 1:1–3; 1 Peter 1:19–20; Revelation 13:8.

[11] Isaiah 53:10.

THE GOD WHO LEADS HISTORY

God has given us the example of Jesus so we will have the confidence necessary to take up our own cross. The question is do we know God like this? Do we know the God who will lead His people into great tribulation?

The real issue is our knowledge of God, and if we do not know God like this, we will be unable to communicate this knowledge of God to others, and our discipleship will be lacking.

This issue is not unique to the life of Jesus. For example, the books of Genesis, Job, and Habakkuk all confront us with this reality. Joseph was betrayed, sold into slavery, falsely accused, falsely imprisoned, and forgotten. Through his trial, he responded correctly, and yet his suffering continued. When his trial was over, he did not say, "God redeemed my trial"; instead, he said three times, "It was not you who sent me here but God."[12]

The book of Job is shocking because God, not Satan, initiated Job's disaster and his suffering. God referred to Job as "a blameless and upright man who fears God and turns away from evil" and yet handed him over to Satan.[13] The book ends by referring to Job's suffering as the "disaster that YHWH had brought upon him."[14] Habakkuk had a similar experience. He accused God of being silent and absent because Judah was being threatened by a hostile, foreign army. God answered Habakkuk's complaint with the shocking revelation that God was the one stirring up Judah's adversary.[15]

These men did not blame their trouble on the devil, and in the process they confront us with the reality that God will design things we would not have chosen for our own benefit.

We quickly agree the cross was God's wisdom, and we even agree with Job's story, but we often lack the same "clarity" on God's

---

[12] Genesis 45:5–8.

[13] Job 1:6–8; 2:3–6.

[14] Michael L. Brown, *Job: The Faith to Challenge God: A New Translation and Commentary* (Peabody, MA: Hendrickson Academic, 2019), Job 42:11.

[15] For more on this, see the book, *Have You Been Blinded? Facing Your Assumptions about God's Leadership.*

leadership over all history. God continues to do what He has always done, and the end of the age is consistent with God's revealed character. Many people think the end times are a time when Satan does whatever he wants, but that is not what the Bible says. God remains actively involved and sovereign over the situation. The mystery of the coming great tribulation is the culmination of the mystery of suffering and calamity in this age—the mystery that God has chosen to produce glory through our own suffering.

God's leadership is a great mystery. God allows creatures to make real decisions, and they often choose evil. Evil is real, and God will judge it. And yet, God uses the evil of this age to accomplish His purposes.

God handed Jesus over to the powers, and this shows us He's also going to hand His people over to the powers that hate Him the most. It's predetermined. It's preplanned. And it's not accidental, because Jesus was also handed over in a preplanned and predetermined way. We often expect that God will always protect us from suffering, but this is not true. There are times God protects us from the enemy, and there are times God "hands us over" and does not protect us. If we do not understand this, we can easily become offended, but we must face this now. Daniel predicted it,[16] and God Himself was handed over in His crucifixion as the "firstborn" of the saints.[17]

Jesus' suffering is the ultimate example of God handing His people over and not protecting them from evil powers. If the Father handed over Jesus, He may also choose to do the same for the rest of His people. We do not need to seek this kind of suffering, but neither should we be ignorant of what the Bible plainly says. The reality that God sometimes hands His people over is very troubling, but when we look at the cross we discover God does not arbitrarily hand His people over. When He chooses to hand them over, He does it to lead His people to glory and exaltation that do not come another way.

DRINK THE CUP

Jesus' public ministry led Him to a crucial moment in a garden:

---

[16] Daniel 7:25.

[17] Romans 8:29.

> *Then he said to them, "My soul is very sorrowful, even to death; remain here, and watch with me." And going a little farther he fell on his face and prayed, saying, "My Father, if it be possible, let this cup pass from me; nevertheless, not as I will, but as you will." . . . Again, for the second time, he went away and prayed, "My Father, if this cannot pass unless I drink it, your will be done." (Matthew 26:38–39, 42)*

In the Garden of Gethsemane, Jesus had a choice, and He choose to set His own suffering into motion:

> Christ chose suffering, it didn't just happen to him. He chose it as the way to create and perfect the church.[18]

Jesus fully considered the cup the Father set in front of Him, and His first response was, "Is there another way?" Jesus lived to do what He saw the Father doing,[19] so this response indicates the magnitude of what Jesus was facing. Luke's Gospel tells us the agony was so severe Jesus sweat blood.[20] He was fully aware of the joy that would result from the cross,[21] but Jesus was also overwhelmed at everything that would accompany His suffering.

Jesus chose to enter "great tribulation" to fulfill the Father's desire and inherit the joy intended for Him.

Because Jesus is the prototype, the church is also headed for a Matthew 26 moment. Jesus' earthy ministry brought Him to the Garden of Gethsemane, and God's plan for the church is leading us to our own Gethsemane. A day will come in the future when the Father looks at the church and sets the "cup" of the great tribulation in front of us. Like Jesus, we will tremble at the cup, knowing the Bible warns it

---

[18]John Piper, "To Finish the Aim of Christ's Afflictions," https://www.desiringgod.org/messages/to-finish-the-aim-of-christs-afflictions/, accessed November 11, 2020.

[19]John 5:19; 8:28; 9:4; 12:49.

[20]Luke 22:44.

[21]Hebrews 12:2.

is a time unlike any other time,[22] and we will be "handed over" to a man so evil the Bible's primary title for him is simply "the beast."[23]

Jesus' suffering was put into motion by Jesus' own decisions. He was not attacked or surprised. He willingly chose to embrace His own suffering and drink the cup the Lord put in front of Him. The mature church will follow this same path. We will stare at the great tribulation, sweat drops of blood, and then say to the Father, "*Yes*, we will do whatever You ask even if our *yes* sets our own tribulation into motion. Even if You hand us over to the beasts and do not protect us or preserve our lives, we will drink the cup You have put in front of us."

Jesus' earthly ministry led Him to Matthew 26, and God's plan for the church is leading us to a corporate Matthew 26 moment.

Jesus had to say *yes* to an overwhelming cup, but the Father also set the promise of joy before Him. The cup is not only about suffering; it is the tremendous cost necessary to purchase unparalleled joy.

We are the joy the Father set before Jesus, and He is the joy the Father has set before us. Jesus drank a horrible cup to purchase us. The question is what generation will drink a similar, terrible cup to secure His return?

Jesus' glory was incomplete until He chose to drink the cup of His own suffering. That drink set into motion the events that gave Him a glorious, immortal body and exalted Him as a man.[24] The same is true of the church. Our glory is incomplete until we drink the same cup and allow the Father to lead us where we would not go otherwise. When we drink that cup and pass through the great tribulation that Jesus' suffering foreshadowed, we will be exalted like Him and made into a companion compatible to Him.

Paul is the most visible apostle in the New Testament and an example of a man who followed Jesus so wholeheartedly his pursuit of Jesus could be imitated.[25] With this in mind, it is noteworthy that, when

---

[22]Jeremiah 30:7; Daniel 12:1; Joel 2:2; Matthew 24:21.

[23]Daniel 7:7–8; Revelation 11:7; 13:1–8, 12, 14–18; 14:9, 11; 15:2; 16:2, 10, 13; 17:3, 7–8, 11–13, 16–17; 19:19–20; 20:4, 10.

[24]Philippians 2:8–10.

[25]1 Corinthians 4:15–16; 11:1; Ephesians 5:1; Philippians 3:17; 1 Thessalonians 1:6; 2 Thessalonians 3:9; Hebrews 6:12.

Paul was called, the Lord also showed him he must drink a cup of suffering.[26] We often think of that cup as Paul's cup of suffering, and there was a specific assignment for Paul, but he is also an apostolic model to us to drink the cup the Lord puts in front of us.

Jesus drank His cup so we would have our reward. Will we drink the cup for Jesus to receive His reward?

God is leading history, and He will bring about Jesus' return in His time and on His schedule. However, Isaiah 42:10–14 strongly hints that passionate songs and longing for Jesus will set His return into motion.[27] The end of the age will not come until the church faces a Matthew 26 moment and says, "Father, we will drink the cup. Do what You will, we want Jesus back."

God is going to produce a church whose pain over Jesus' absence is greater than her fear of the great tribulation. This will be the Father's great gift to Jesus. And she will see the return of the One her soul dearly loves.

The end of the age will not come until the church comes to a Matthew 26 moment and cries out, "We will drink the cup." The Lord waits for the church to lift that cry, but His desire to return to His people is so great that He will only wait so long until He sets events into motion to provoke that cry. God waited thousands of years for His Son to come and drink the cup. He has been working for two thousands years for a corporate people to drink their cup.

We rejoice in Jesus' suffering for our sakes but rarely consider that He endured our suffering to give us courage so we would follow Him and embrace the same path of suffering.

There are sufferings that are Jesus' alone to bear. For example, He alone can secure atonement. Our suffering is not identical to His, but we are called to embrace the same path to exaltation. Jesus' call to take up our cross as well as the apostles' embrace of suffering[28] clearly demonstrate Jesus' suffering foreshadowed our own path.

---

[26]Acts 9:16.

[27]This does not mean we control the timing of Jesus' return, but in His sovereign leadership God will use His people to accomplish what He wants.

[28]Acts 14:22; Romans 8:17–18; Philippians 1:29; 3:10–11; Hebrews 2:10; 5:8; 1 Peter 2:19–21; 4:13–14, 19; 5:9–10; Revelation 2:10.

Jesus overcame the root of human sin, and He is the firstborn of a people who must also defeat that sin.[29] The root of all human sin is the decision to evaluate God and choose our evaluation over His. All sin flows from this. Jesus overcame this sin in the garden. He perceived the horror of the cup but chose the Father's will over His own evaluation of the cup. He had more confidence in the Father than what He saw and perceived in that moment.

Jesus came to maturity through the things He suffered,[30] and the same will be true for His people because Jesus is the firstborn of many sons of glory.[31] Like Him, they will drink the cup. Drinking the cup does not mean pursuing suffering. (There were times the apostles made decisions to avoid certain situations.[32]) It means being willing to drink the cup the Father puts in front of you and choosing His evaluation over your own. It means letting Him do whatever He wants including handing you over. You do not seek suffering, but you release yourself into the Father's design over your life even if you will be led somewhere you would not go.[33]

When you drink the cup, you drink knowing it may lead to your death. God may not protect you or preserve your life. When Jesus drank the cup, the Father did not protect Him. He handed Him over, and the Father may do the same to us. However, we can be confident that, if God hands us over to suffering, our momentary affliction will produce an everlasting reward.[34]

We are heading toward a moment when God will ask us to drink the cup. When the corporate church says yes knowing God will hand us over, we will be the mature "Bride" prepared for our scarred and slain "groom."

---

[29] For more on this, see the book, *Have You Been Blinded? Facing Your Assumptions about God's Leadership*.

[30] Hebrews 5:8.

[31] Romans 8:29.

[32] Acts 20:3; 2 Corinthians 11:32–33.

[33] John 21:18.

[34] 2 Corinthians 4:17.

Jesus' suffering did not begin until He drank the cup, and the great tribulation will not come until the mature church also chooses to "drink the cup." Like Jesus, the end-time church will:

- Fully grasp what is coming through her knowledge of the Word.
- Feel the full weight of her decision.
- Soberly and honestly say, "Not my will, but Your will be done."

Across the global church, God is stirring up a growing interest in studying what the Bible says about the end times in a biblical and responsible way. He is informing His people to prepare us for the coming Matthew 26 moment. This mature church will be the John 17 witness that Jesus prayed for. She will follow His path and in the process become the undeniable evidence that He exists.

Are you discipling people to drink the cup the Lord puts in front of them?

ISRAEL

The cup Jesus drank was a cup the prophets had spoken of. It was a cup of sin and rebellion, but first of all it was connected to Israel's sin and disobedience. Jesus not only took humanity's punishment, He willingly took Israel's punishment. He identified with the sinful to become a means of salvation, and His suffering unfolded in and around Jerusalem.[35]

People often discuss Israel's end-time trouble, also known as "Jacob's trouble,"[36] as if it is merely prophetic information. However, if you are grafted into Israel, you are not only grafted into Israel's blessings—you are also grafted into Israel's suffering. The Bible predicts the age will end with great trouble around Jerusalem,[37] and in that moment the church will be called, like Jesus, to identify with Israel and share in Israel's suffering to be part of Israel's reconciliation to God.

---

[35] Isaiah 51:17; 53:4–6, 11–12; Jeremiah 25:15.

[36] Jeremiah 30:7.

[37] Psalm 98; Isaiah 13:8; 34; Jeremiah 30:7; Daniel 7:21–22; Daniel 12:1; Joel 3:1–16; Zechariah 12:2–3; 13:8–9; 14:–4, 9, 11; Jeremiah 30:5–7; Matthew 24:15–30; Revelation 11:2; 12:13.

Jesus was without sin, but He identified with us and more specifically with Israel. He chose to drink the cup of Israel's sin to secure redemption. If we are like Jesus, and grafted into Israel, we will also willingly endure suffering *with* Israel so that Israel may hear the good news of salvation and her God. This is natural for Jewish believers, but gentile believers will also willingly identify with Israel at the end of the age. People not originally part of Israel's story or subject to Israel's trouble will become a living representative of God's love and affection for Israel. Those of us who are Gentiles will willingly enter into Israel's suffering for the sake of her salvation.

If we have truly been grafted into Israel,[38] *we will be asked to drink Israel's end-time cup of suffering.*

Jesus alone secured atonement, but the end-time suffering of the church will be salvific in the sense her suffering will be an extravagant demonstration of love that will provoke Israel and others to cry out to the God of Israel for salvation. Have we considered that God loves Israel enough, not only to sacrifice His Son, but also lead His gentile people to become a similar offering on Israel's behalf at the end of the age?

---

[38] Romans 11:17.

THE FATHER'S DREAM

It is time for us to align our dreams with the Father's dream.

Jesus has been waiting 2,000 years for His reward, and the Father is looking for a people who are so moved with affection for Him and what He has done that they will say, *"Father I don't really care how my inheritance turns out in this age. I am not fulfilled until He is fulfilled. Give your Son His inheritance. Give Him what He has waited for. I am not content until He is content."*

We do conferences and write books about how to be fulfilled. It's not all wrong, but why do we expect to be completely fulfilled in this age? Jesus has been waiting thousands of years for His reward and His fulfillment. He is still waiting, so why do we expect everything in seventy years?

The Father is going to mature His church.

The Father is going to produce a people who are not content with Jesus' absence. They will be gripped by the desire for His return. They will not be obsessed with charts and graphs; they will be preoccupied with the Father's desire to give His Son an inheritance.

This people will disciple. They will eagerly engage in missions. They will joyfully sacrifice. They will do everything they can in their strength to give Jesus His reward. Their desire will know no limits—they will do everything they can even if it means enduring the great tribulation.

We must not overlook the difficulty of the great tribulation. Scripture warns it is like no other time in history.[1] However, a church is going to emerge that misses Jesus more than she fears the great tribulation. This mature church will be the Father's gift to the Son—a

---

[1] Matthew 24:21; Jeremiah 30:7; Daniel 12:1; Joel 2:2.

bride made ready. There is a sense in which the return of Jesus waits for a church to come to this place.

Jesus deserves the nations. He deserves everything He paid such a high and terrible price for. We are told the return of Jesus is like a wedding and Jesus returns when His Bride has "made herself ready" (Revelation 19). No groom wants to show up to a wedding to marry a disinterested bride. Every groom is hoping for a bride who is eager filled with desire—a bride who has been longing the day and eagerly preparing.

The Father is going to give Jesus this kind of people, and this is what our discipleship should be producing. If it is not producing this, we need to ask some serious questions and make some adjustments.

Forget your calling. Forget your reward. Align with the Father. Give your life to see Jesus receive His reward. I guarantee, if you align your life's vision with the Father's desire, He will take care of you in ways you cannot imagine. You will not lose anything of what He has for you.

WHY EMBRACE SUFFERING?

Many people endure suffering for the hope or a reward or the sake of a cause, but Christian suffering is different from other suffering. We embrace suffering primarily for the purpose of transformation because our God is a suffering God. God is revealed at many times in many ways, but the cross is the only moment in eternity when God has been naked and fully exposed. The message is clear: *This is God unveiled. This is who He really is.* God is a "lamb slain" forever.

God's core identity was revealed in the context of His suffering, but He is not simply one who suffered for a moment. In His suffering, He revealed who He is all the time.

In our suffering, we become like our God, and this is what makes Christian suffering different from any other kind of suffering. We are not simply seeking a reward; we are embracing the difficult process of being made into His image. He has suffered more than any other person, and He continues to suffer *willingly* for the sake of His creation. He is looking for a people who embrace His suffering and become like Him. That is why we suffer.

Suffering does not always make sense in the moment, and we are not a people who seek out suffering. Yet, the mature church will choose to suffer because our God chooses to suffer. The cross is the most dramatic moment of His suffering, but it reveals who He is all the time, and it presents the image He wants to transform us into.

The end of our suffering is *transformation* and *joy*. Jesus embraced suffering for the joy of a people who are like Him. We embrace suffering to become a people like Him. This led Paul to describe suffering as a gift:

> *For it has been granted to you that for the sake of Christ you should not only believe in him but also suffer for his sake. (Philippians 1:29)*

Or to quote Richard Wurmbrand who suffered tremendously:

> If suffering were offered to you as a gift, would you accept it?[2]

We don't *pursue* it, but will we *embrace* the suffering that makes us like the Divine Slain Lamb?

DIVINE SUFFERING

When Jesus chose to share in our sufferings, He opened up a mystery: The sufferings of man are also the sufferings of God.

> *For as we share abundantly in Christ's sufferings, so through Christ we share abundantly in comfort too. (2 Corinthians 1:5)*

When we suffer, we share in *Jesus'* suffering, not simply our own suffering. Our suffering is an experience of and identification with God's own suffering, and so suffering fashions us into the likeness of God in a unique way.

As Isaiah said:

> *In all their affliction he was afflicted, and the angel of his presence saved them; in his love and in his pity he redeemed them; he lifted them up and carried them all the days of old. (63:9)*

And again in Hebrews:

---

[2] John Piper, "Filling Up What Is Lacking in Christ's Afflictions," https://www.desiringgod.org/messages/filling-up-what-is-lacking-in-christs-afflictions/, accessed November 12, 2020.

> *For it was fitting that he, for whom and by whom all things exist, in bringing many sons to glory, should make the founder of their salvation perfect through suffering. (2:10)*

We do not enjoy suffering or seek it out. There were times Paul avoided suffering and expressed the difficulty of his own suffering,[3] but he understood it was an identification with Jesus. Following Jesus' example, we also embrace suffering for the sake of the body:

> *If we are afflicted, it is for your comfort and salvation; and if we are comforted, it is for your comfort, which you experience when you patiently endure the same sufferings that we suffer. (2 Corinthians 1:6)*

Jesus consecrated Himself and suffered for the sake of His people,[4] and there are times we are called to follow His path and suffer for the sake of what it will produce in a community.

SURVIVING BETRAYAL

Jesus chose to be handed over for suffering, and He was handed over through a painful betrayal.[5] Jesus' betrayal is also part of the foreshadowing of His suffering because Satan "entered" Judas, and the only other man that seems to have that sort of relationship with Satan is the antichrist.[6] If Jesus was handed over for His suffering through betrayal, it is likely the same will be true for the end-time church.

Betrayal is not unique to Jesus—it is one of the most painful things believers must pass through.

Betrayal is not an act by an enemy—it is a painful act by one who was considered to be a friend. Not only will God hand us over at times to suffering, He may hand us over through betrayal as He did His Son. Obviously, only one generation will pass through the end-time challenge that Jesus' death foreshadows, but betrayal is one of the more difficult challenges in the Christian life.

---

[3] Philippians 3:8–10; 1 Corinthians 4:9–13; 2 Corinthians 11:23–27; 2 Timothy 4:6.

[4] John 17:19.

[5] Matthew 26:49–40; Luke 22:47–48.

[6] Luke 22:3; Revelation 13:2.

We cannot read the story of Jesus' own betrayal and then become offended when the same happens to us. If it happened to Jesus, it will happen to us. Betrayal is so prominent in the biblical story that, it not only caused Jesus' execution, it set the redemptive story into motion. Somewhere in the beginning, a powerful being named Satan betrayed God. Then, in an ultimate act of betrayal, he came into the garden and turned God's prize creature against Him.

God's betrayal in Genesis 3 set God's purposes into motion. Do you have courage to face the fact that betrayal could also play a part in God's divine purpose for you? What if God hands us over to betrayal? What if He allows us to share in His own betrayal? Will we survive? Will we make it? Will we trust His wise leadership? Or will the pain overcome us?

Betrayal is one of the biggest tests most believers face, and it will be a significant end-time test. Are you discipling people to expect betrayal and to endure betrayal with a clean heart?

Accusation is the basis of betrayal, and it is so central to the enemy's schemes that Satan is referred to as the "accuser of the brethren."[7] Satan accuses us in the heavens, and yet God rejects his accusation and instead proclaims Zechariah 3 over His people:

> *And the LORD said to Satan, "The LORD rebuke you, O Satan! The LORD who has chosen Jerusalem rebuke you! Is not this a brand plucked from the fire?" And the angel said to those who were standing before him, "Remove the filthy garments from him." And to him he said, "Behold, I have taken your iniquity away from you, and I will clothe you with pure vestments." And I said, "Let them put a clean turban on his head." So they put a clean turban on his head and clothed him with garments. And the angel of the LORD was standing by. (vv. 2, 4–5)*

God does not "betray" His people even when Satan's accusations against us have a measure of truth. In Zechariah 3, Joshua's garments really were stained, but God resists accusations and wrong narratives about His people. He instead qualifies them. We are called to do the same.

---

[7] Revelation 12:10.

We *must* resolve our accusations against each other, or we can become instruments of betrayal ourselves. We tend to avoid conflict, but this allows accusations to foster into betrayal, so Jesus *commanded* us to seek resolution when conflict and questions arise.[8]

Eve and Adam fell because they believed Satan's accusations against God, and that is perhaps the greatest accusation of all. If you seek to follow Jesus and follow His example, Satan's accusations will come, "God just wants you to suffer. He does not care about you. If He really loved you, He would protect you. He would have kept you from betrayal." The fruit in the garden looked good, and these accusations may feel right in the moment, but they are deadly accusations intended to prevent our glory and cause God pain.

The mature church is going to consider Satan's accusations and then drink the cup God puts in front of her anyway.

When we choose the cup God puts in front of us, we reject the sin of the garden—we deny the fundamental human sin. The mature church must not only reject accusations against each other, but must release all our accusations against God.

Revelation 12 tells us that Satan is going to be dislodged from his place of accusation in the heavens. He was defeated on the cross by a man who refused accusations against God and chose instead to obey His Father in the most costly way possible. Perhaps Satan's future fall in Revelation 12 will come when the end-time church chooses to drink the cup and reject every accusation against God.

Are we discipling people to actively resist accusation against one another and accusations against God Himself?

God's Patient Process

Accusation, betrayal, and suffering are very heavy subjects. They are difficult and painful to endure. With that in mind, we must remember God is patient with us. As we cooperate with Him, He will mature us over time. The thought of enduring suffering as Jesus did may be completely overwhelming. *Don't give up.* As you embrace a path of discipleship, you will be transformed.

God's demands are incredibly high, but He is also incredibly patient. The stories of the Bible demonstrate He is not discouraged by

---

[8] Matthew 18:15–20.

our growth. He enjoys working with weak people, even people who have made massive mistakes. When you endure accusations, betrayal, and suffering, God understands your pain.[9] When you are prone to accuse others, He will confront your sin and discipline you because of His intense love for you.[10]

Even Jesus looked at the cup of suffering and asked the Father if there was another way. God does not mind if we struggle with His leadership, but we must allow Him to remove accusation from our hearts and lives with a bold confidence in His goodness regardless of where He leads us.

We do not have to understand everything. We simply need to come to the place where we say, "Not my will but Your will be done," when the Father leads us to a place we would not naturally go. When we come to this maturity, we dethrone Satan's influence.

God's process is not the same for every person, and we should not seek out suffering or betrayal, but if God had to enter into His glory through betrayal, pain, self-sacrifice, and death, we should not be surprised when similar afflictions come our way. This core issue is not the expression of our suffering; it is our willingness to drink the cup He puts in front of us and follow His leadership wherever He goes.

The Father wants to give us a dimension of glory that only He can produce. That glory will comes through His process. His ways are not our ways.

---

[9] Isaiah 63:9; Hebrews 4:15–16.

[10] Proverbs 3:12; Hebrews 12:6–8.

THE REVELATION OF JESUS AND HIS PEOPLE

Far too many people think the book of Revelation is mostly about the beast and suffering. The book of Revelation contains very sobering warnings that must be taken seriously, but these are not the dominant theme of the book. The main theme of the book is the revelation of Jesus in majesty through the events of the second coming. If we do not read Revelation and all prophecy with this in mind, we will miss the main point of these prophecies because prophecy exists to reveal Jesus.[1]

For example, if you consider a few stats in the book of Revelation, the dominant theme becomes immediately apparent:

- Jesus is mentioned in 127 verses.[2]
- Satan is mentioned in 28 verses.[3]
- The beast (antichrist) is mentioned in 32 verses.[4]

---

[1] Revelation 19:10.

[2] Revelation 1:1–2, 5–18, 20; 2:1–10, 12–14, 16–28; 3:1–5, 7–12, 14–16, 18–21; 5:5–10, 12–13; 6:1, 3, 5, 7, 9, 12, 16–17; 7:9–10, 14, 17; 8:1; 11:8, 15; 12:10–11, 17; 13:8; 14:1, 4, 10, 12, 14, 15–16; 15:3; 16:15; 17:6, 14; 19:7, 9–16, 19, 21; 20:4, 6; 21:2, 9, 14, 22–23, 27; 22:1, 3, 7, 12–13, 16–17, 20, 21.

[3] Revelation 2:9–10, 13, 24; 3:9; 12:3–4, 7–17; 13:1–2, 4; 16:13; 20:2–3, 7–10.

[4] Revelation 11:7; 13:1–8, 12, 14–15, 17–18; 14:9, 11; 15:2; 16:2, 10, 13; 17:3, 7–8, 11–13, 16–17; 19:19–20; 20:4, 10.

If the book of Revelation is primarily about the revelation of Jesus,[5] then it must also be about the revelation of His people. This is precisely what we find in the book of Revelation. In every passage where Jesus appears, a people appear with Him. This correlation is part of the message of the book: Jesus will be glorified, and a people are part of that process.

We need to briefly summarize this pattern in Revelation because we need to learn to read the Bible's predictions about the end times the way they were intended to be read. We must not minimize the trouble, but we must put the trouble in context. The trouble of the end times is not meaningless, nor is it a temporary triumph of evil. It is part of the Father's intentional, but mysterious, plan to reveal His Son and His people in a spectacular way.

REVELATION 1–3

Revelation 1 is the introduction to the entire book. It carries special significance because it summarizes the main message of the book. As we have mentioned, the book begins by plainly summarizing the main purpose of the book:

> *The revelation of Jesus Christ, which God gave him to show to his servants the things that must soon take place. . . . (1:1)*

This book contains a revelation of Jesus given by God so that Jesus' people can understand it and cooperate with God's plan.

As the introduction continues, John describes who Jesus is and what He has done. These descriptions emphasize Jesus' beauty, and in verses 5–6, we find John's first statement summarizing what Jesus has done:

> *To him who loves us and has freed us from our sins by his blood and made us a kingdom, priests to his God and Father, to him be glory and dominion forever and ever. Amen.*

John could have begun His summary of Jesus' glory with many different descriptions. For example, it would have been reasonable to speak about the revelation of Jesus' majesty in creation because He

---

[5]Revelation 1:1.

made all things.[6] John could have said many things about Jesus, and he began by saying that Jesus has formed a people. John started with this because it is the most spectacular thing Jesus has done.

A few verses later, John described an encounter with Jesus. In the encounter, he saw Jesus in His beauty, and John could not stand. In the context of Revelation 1, this encounter carries a message: When Jesus is revealed at the end of the age, He will be spectacular. Those who think they know Him best will be unable to endure the glory of His person and will fall at His feet as though dead.

When John encountered Jesus, He was standing among lamp stands, which represented churches.[7] The message is clear: The glory of Jesus that will be seen at the end of the age will be revealed *among His people*. To use Paul's analogy,[8] the "Head" will be with the "body" because Jesus' glory is not only associated with His people, it is found *among His people*.

Jesus gave John a series of messages for the churches. These messages complete the introduction of the book, and they are found in Revelation 2–3. Before Jesus describes the end-time drama or speaks about the beast, He focuses on His church.

The introduction of Revelation focuses almost entirely on Jesus and His people, indicating the main theme of the book is Jesus and His people.

Jesus' introductory message to the churches contains several astounding statements:

> *"He who has an ear, let him hear what the Spirit says to the churches. To the one who conquers I will grant to eat of the tree of life, which is in the paradise of God." (2:7)*

> *"Be faithful unto death, and I will give you the crown of life. . . . The one who conquers will not be hurt by the second death." (vv. 10–11)*

> *"He who has an ear, let him hear what the Spirit says to the churches. To the one who conquers I will give some of the hidden manna, and I will*

---

[6] John 1:1–5; Colossians 1:16; Hebrews 1:3.

[7] Revelation 1:12–13, 20.

[8] 1 Corinthians 12:18–26; Ephesians 1:23; 4:15–16; Colossians 1:18, 24.

> *give him a white stone, with a new name written on the stone that no one knows except the one who receives it." (v. 17)*
>
> *"The one who conquers and who keeps my works until the end, to him I will give authority over the nations, and he will rule them with a rod of iron, as when earthen pots are broken in pieces, even as I myself have received authority from my Father." (vv. 26–27)*
>
> *"The one who conquers will be clothed thus in white garments, and I will never blot his name out of the book of life. I will confess his name before my Father and before his angels." (3:5)*
>
> *"Behold, I will make those of the synagogue of Satan who say that they are Jews and are not, but lie—behold, I will make them come and bow down before your feet, and they will learn that I have loved you." (v. 9)*
>
> *"The one who conquers, I will make him a pillar in the temple of my God. Never shall he go out of it, and I will write on him the name of my God, and the name of the city of my God, the new Jerusalem, which comes down from my God out of heaven, and my own new name." (v. 12)*
>
> *"I counsel you to buy from me gold refined by fire, so that you may be rich, and white garments so that you may clothe yourself and the shame of your nakedness may not be seen, and salve to anoint your eyes, so that you may see. . . . The one who conquers, I will grant him to sit with me on my throne, as I also conquered and sat down with my Father on his throne. He who has an ear, let him hear what the Spirit says to the churches." (vv. 18, 21–22)*

We could summarize these chapters by saying Jesus wants to share His glory with a people. Jesus lists several rewards He wants to give the church, and these rewards are essentially the reward of becoming like Jesus and being exalted with Him. Revelation 2–3 contains important instructions to share Jesus' glory.

The first subject of the book of Revelation is the beauty of Jesus,[9] and the first message given in the book is a series of exhortations to be faithful and live carefully in order to share in Jesus' glory and be exalted with Him when He returns.

---

[9]Revelation 1:5–18.

The book of Revelation is introduced as the revelation of Jesus and a people, but that is only the beginning.

REVELATION 4–5

Before John is shown any end-time details, He is invited to "come up"[10] and see a stunning revelation of God. It begins with a description of God on His throne, but as John continues to gaze, the vision becomes more specific: He sees Jesus as the Divine Slain Lamb enthroned over all creation. This encounter sets the tone for the rest of the book by emphasizing Jesus' beauty, majesty, supremacy, and sovereignty. All the end-time details that follow this part of the book should be read in light of this encounter.

As the Lamb is given a scroll to set into motion God's end-time plan, heavenly creatures fall on their faces and erupt in a chorus of worship:

> *And when he had taken the scroll, the four living creatures and the twenty-four elders fell down before the Lamb, each holding a harp, and golden bowls full of incense, which are the prayers of the saints. And they sang a new song, saying, "Worthy are you to take the scroll and to open its seals, for you were slain, and by your blood you ransomed people for God from every tribe and language and people and nation, and you have made them a kingdom and priests to our God, and they shall reign on the earth." (5:8–10)*

They sing of the glory of the Lamb because He has done the impossible: *He has ransomed a people for God and transformed them into a kingdom of priests who will reign with God.* The song of Revelation 5 is an exposition of Revelation 1. John introduced Jesus' majesty with the fact that He had redeemed a people, and heaven's worship began with the same accolade.

In fact, in this throne room scene, the entire chorus of praise specifically directed at Jesus centers on His formation of a people who can stand with Him in the heavenly realm (priests) and rule with Him (kingdom). These heavenly creatures saw the beauty and majesty of Jesus and then responded with the highest accolade they could give Him. They praised Him for His ability to form a people like Himself.

---

[10] Revelation 4:1.

The heavenly chorus of praise indicates the redeemed people of God are the most spectacular thing Jesus has done from heaven's perspective.

To further emphasize the majesty of Jesus' people, John tells us the elders have golden bowls filled with the prayers of the saints. Because of Jesus, there is a people whose words are now captured by the highest beings in heaven. People are now speaking in the place of God's government and ruling with Him. It's an incredible picture of the exalted place of Jesus' people.

The question is do we think about the people of God the way heaven does?

Some people may fear discussing the exalted people of God will produce pride, but it will not. In fact, the opposite is true. When we minimize the glory of Jesus' people, it fosters pride because we imagine our glory is connected to our strength, achievements, or abilities. When we see the true majesty of Jesus' people, it is obvious no human could exalt himself to this place. The fact humans who were born fallen—enemies of God—can be exalted to this place demonstrates the majesty of Jesus in a profound way.

Revelation 1 contains the first description of Jesus in His majesty on the earth, and Jesus appears among His people. Revelation 5 contains the first description of Jesus' majesty in the heavens, and Jesus' majesty is in context to His people.

Heaven worships Jesus for His ability to form a people—do we?

Revelation 6–7

Revelation 1–3 is the first scene that reveals Jesus' beauty on the earth, Revelation 4–5 is a second scene that reveals His majesty in the heavens, and Revelation 6–7 is a third scene that reveals His sovereignty over creation. In the first two scenes, Jesus' majesty was accompanied by a revelation of His people, and the same thing occurs in Revelation 6–7.

In Revelation 6, Jesus is breaking seals on a document that He alone is worthy to open. As these seals break, dramatic events unfold under Jesus' leadership and control. The chapter emphasizes the theme of Jesus as the exalted Divine Man who is ruling over creation.

As Jesus exercises His dominion over creation, John sees the martyrs:

When he opened the fifth seal, I saw under the altar the souls of those who had been slain for the word of God and for the witness they had borne. They cried out with a loud voice, "O Sovereign Lord, holy and true, how long before you will judge and avenge our blood on those who dwell on the earth?" Then they were each given a white robe and told to rest a little longer, until the number of their fellow servants and their brothers should be complete, who were to be killed as they themselves had been. (6:9–11)

The martyrs are told to be patient with the process because Jesus' end-time plan is going to vindicate and exalt them. John then sees 144,000 people marked to be kept and saved by Jesus, and then he sees something spectacular. In the first two scenes revealing Jesus' beauty, His people were described, but this time there is more than a mention of the exalted people. John actually *sees them*, and they are breathtaking:

After this I looked, and behold, a great multitude that no one could number, from every nation, from all tribes and peoples and languages, standing before the throne and before the Lamb, clothed in white robes, with palm branches in their hands, and crying out with a loud voice, "Salvation belongs to our God who sits on the throne, and to the Lamb!" (7:9–10)

When the angels see the end-time church, they are overcome and fall on their faces with shouts of praise:

And all the angels were standing around the throne and around the elders and the four living creatures, and they fell on their faces before the throne and worshiped God, saying, "Amen! Blessing and glory and wisdom and thanksgiving and honor and power and might be to our God forever and ever! Amen." (7:11–12)

As in Revelation 5, angels fall on their faces because Jesus has produced a people. The angels' response reveals quite a bit about the end-time church. Again, we have to ask: Do we see the church this way, and are we anticipating this end-time event?

As the angels magnified God, one of the elders spoke to John:

Then one of the elders addressed me, saying, "Who are these, clothed in white robes, and from where have they come?" I said to him, "Sir, you know." And he said to me, "These are the ones coming out of the great tribulation. They have washed their robes and made them white in the blood of the Lamb. Therefore they are before the throne of God, and serve him day and night in his temple. . . . For the Lamb in the midst of the throne will be their shepherd, and he will guide them to springs of living water, and God will wipe away every tear from their eyes." (vv. 13–17)

This elder wanted to make sure John understood why the angels fell on their faces in worship. John had to understand God is producing a people, they will emerge in the end-times, they will proclaim the glory of God, they will come from every people, they will be a great multitude, and this plan will provoke angels to worship. John carefully recorded this conversation with the elder so we would know the nature of the end-time church.

The message is clear: Jesus' end-time leadership is going to produce a majestic people. When He is exalted, they will appear with Him and be like Him.

The end-time people of God are so stunning it causes angels to fall on their faces and worship God.

REVELATION 12–13

The next main appearance of Jesus occurs in Revelation 12. This chapter uses apocalyptic imagery to summarize God's redemptive plan, and Jesus appears as the "Male Child"[11] born to rule. The chapter focuses on the rage of a dragon (Satan) against the Male Child (Jesus). Jesus is carried away, so Satan wages war on Jesus' people.[12]

Satan is called the "accuser of the brethren" because accusation is his primary weapon against the people of God. He does not want the church to know who they really are.[13] However, the people of God overcome Him by the blood of the Lamb and the word of their testimony. They are faithful unto death. Like Jesus, they overcome Satan through obedience unto suffering.[14] When Satan is thrown down

---

[11] Revelation 12:5.

[12] Revelation 12:4–5, 17.

[13] Revelation 12:10.

[14] Revelation 12:11.

to the earth in this chapter, he rages against God by trying to destroy and eliminate the people who belong to Jesus.

Revelation 12 describes Satan's rage against God's purposes, but it is similar to the other scriptures we have considered because, once again, Jesus and His people are deeply connected. Satan's rage against Jesus is expressed through rage and accusation against His people.

Accusation is a tool that is used to keep someone from being seen for who they truly are. You may accuse individuals to give them a negative image of themselves, or you accuse them to others so others will not desire them. Either way, you accuse someone when you are threatened by who they are or who they will become.

The end-time drama in Revelation 12 shows Satan does not want the church to know who she is, fears who she will become, and wages war on Jesus by seeking to destroy His people. Again, there is a profound connection between Jesus and His people as well as strong hints at their glory and exaltation with Him.

Revelation 13 predicts the terrible beast[15] who comes at the end of the age will set up an image and require people to take his "mark."[16] The beast, his image, and his mark are a counterfeit of John 17. Jesus will have a people at the end of the age who are His image, and the beast will also have a people who are transformed into his image. The transformation of the beast's people into his image will be so profound they will be unable to repent afterward.[17] The beast's followers will become like him just as the mature church becomes increasingly like Jesus. The image of Jesus *and* the image of Satan will be fully revealed in two humans and their corresponding people.

REVELATION 14

When Jesus appears standing on Mount Zion in Revelation 14, He appears with a people:

> *Then I looked, and behold, on Mount Zion stood the Lamb, and with him 144,000 who had his name and his Father's name written on their*

---

[15] Antichrist.

[16] Revelation 13:16–17.

[17] Revelation 14:9–10.

> *foreheads. . . . It is these who follow the Lamb wherever he goes. These have been redeemed from mankind as firstfruits for God and the Lamb. (vv. 1–4)*

Revelation 14 ends with another vision of Jesus ready to judge the earth, and the first thing He does is gather a people from the nations:

> *Then I looked, and behold, a white cloud, and seated on the cloud one like a son of man, with a golden crown on his head, and a sharp sickle in his hand. And another angel came out of the temple, calling with a loud voice to him who sat on the cloud, "Put in your sickle, and reap, for the hour to reap has come, for the harvest of the earth is fully ripe." So he who sat on the cloud swung his sickle across the earth, and the earth was reaped. (vv. 14–16)*

This is the great end-time "harvest" of people out of the nations.[18] This is the last thing Jesus does in the book of Revelation before He begins to release His wrath and His final judgments because once Jesus gets the people He wants, this age will have served its purpose, and it will come to a close.

REVELATION 17–18

Revelation 17–18 describes an end-time system called "Harlot Babylon" that will be used to bring great deception and suffering. While Jesus does not appear in chapter 17, there are two references to the saints that give us insight into the end-time church.

The saints are described as the "witnesses" of Jesus:

> *And I saw the woman, drunk with the blood of the saints, the blood of the martyrs of Jesus. When I saw her, I marveled greatly. (v. 6)*

This verse summarizes everything we have seen. The word translated *martyrs* can also be translated *witnesses*[19] because it is a word that describes legal witnesses. In a courtroom, witnesses are evidence of what is true, and the same is true for the church. This is an indicator Jesus' prayer will be answered. At the end of the age, the church will

---

[18] Revelation 5:9; 7:9.

[19] *Witnesses* is used in the New American Standard Bible and the New Living Translation.

become the undeniable evidence (witnesses) of Jesus in the earth. That witness will be so compelling this evil system will kill saints.

Jesus is mentioned one other time in the chapter:

> *"He is Lord of lords and King of kings, and those with him are called and chosen and faithful." (v. 14)*

Jesus is presented as the exalted "Lord of lords and King of kings," and He does not stand alone. He has a people with Him.

REVELATION 19–20

We have already discussed Revelation 19, so we will only briefly mention it here. Revelation 19 contains a dramatic description of the return of Jesus as He executes judgment on the beast and his armies who have enslaved the earth. The chapter begins with a shout of praise because the Bride has made herself ready, and it is time for the marriage of the Lamb to His people:

> *"Let us rejoice and exult and give him the glory, for the marriage of the Lamb has come, and his Bride has made herself ready; it was granted her to clothe herself with fine linen, bright and pure"—for the fine linen is the righteous deeds of the saints. And the angel said to me, "Write this: Blessed are those who are invited to the marriage supper of the Lamb." And he said to me, "These are the true words of God." (vv. 7–9)*

The message is simple and powerful: When Jesus' church is ready to be joined to Him, the age will end. Once Jesus has His companion, there is no more need for this age. It will have served its purpose by revealing God and forming a people for Him.

When Jesus appears, He releases His judgments to liberate the earth from evil, and He enthrones a people with Him:

> *Then I saw thrones, and seated on them were those to whom the authority to judge was committed. Also I saw the souls of those who had been beheaded for the testimony of Jesus and for the word of God, and those who had not worshiped the beast or its image and had not received its mark on their foreheads or their hands. . . . Blessed and holy is the one who shares in the first resurrection! Over such the second death has no power, but they will be priests of God and of Christ, and they will reign with him for a thousand years. (20:4–6)*

Yet again, Jesus appears with His people.

REVELATION 21–22

Revelation 21–22 is the great climax of the book and the final two chapters of the Bible. These chapters describe a new creation and the restoration of all things as Jesus rules on the earth and prepares the way for the heavenly city to descend with God coming to dwell on the earth. These chapters are like the last scenes in a movie. They are a celebration—a resolution—to all the drama that has come before. The age has ended, and the story now turns to a new time—a new age.

As the next age begins, there is a great celebration because God finally has what He wanted: *a companion:*

> *And I heard a loud voice from the throne saying, "Behold, the dwelling place of God is with man. He will dwell with them, and they will be his people, and God himself will be with them as their God. He will wipe away every tear from their eyes, and death shall be no more, neither shall there be mourning, nor crying, nor pain anymore, for the former things have passed away." And he who was seated on the throne said, "Behold, I am making all things new." Also he said, "Write this down, for these words are trustworthy and true. . . . The one who conquers will have this heritage, and I will be his God and he will be my son." (21:3–7)*
>
> *Blessed are those who wash their robes, so that they may have the right to the tree of life and that they may enter the city by the gates. (22:14)*

God's plan is so deeply connected to His people that the walls and the foundations of the heavenly city have human names written on them:

> *It had a great, high wall, with twelve gates, and at the gates twelve angels, and on the gates the names of the twelve tribes of the sons of Israel were inscribed. . . . And the wall of the city had twelve foundations, and on them were the twelve names of the twelve apostles of the Lamb. (Revelation 21:12–14)*

The heavenly city is the dwelling place of God, but He established it as a place for Him to dwell *with a people.*

THE FINAL GLIMPSE OF JESUS AND HIS COMPANION

The book of Revelation contains several dramatic predictions about the coming beast and the great tribulation at the end of the age, but the main theme of the book is the unveiling of Jesus. If we miss that theme, we miss the main message of the book. We need to soberly consider everything in the book, but we must read the book the way John (and the Lord) intended us to read it.

As we have seen, Jesus' exaltation is directly connected to a people. Revelation contains repeated visions of Jesus' beauty, and in each of those visions, we see Jesus accompanied by a people. We began this book seeing that the mature church is a major end-time theme. When we compare the significance of this theme in the New Testament with people's grasp of it, it is potentially the most neglected end-time theme. The book of Revelation describes the end-time church as overcoming and faithful to Jesus even unto death. It is clear something significant has happened. The church has come to maturity in the midst of the end-time crisis.

The book of Revelation describes the fulfillment of Jesus' prayer in John 17.

As John wrote his vision down, he was likely amazed as he described the glory of the fulfillment of the prayer he had heard Jesus pray so long before.

A Present Demonstration of a Future Reality

From the very beginning, God has called His people to be a present demonstration of a future reality, and this display will reach a crescendo just before Jesus returns.

When we considered the seriousness of the revelation of Jesus, we briefly described Paul's dispute with Peter in Antioch. This event is only found in a few verses so it is easy to overlook its significance, but it goes right to the heart of what the church really is.

Paul summarized the conflict in Galatians:

> *But when Cephas came to Antioch, I opposed him to his face, because he stood condemned. For before certain men came from James, he was eating with the Gentiles; but when they came he drew back and separated himself, fearing the circumcision party. And the rest of the Jews acted hypocritically along with him, so that even Barnabas was led astray by their hypocrisy. But when I saw that their conduct was not in step with the truth of the gospel, I said to Cephas before them all, "If you, though a Jew, live like a Gentile and not like a Jew, how can you force the Gentiles to live like Jews?" (Galatians 2:11–14)*

This confrontation was incredibly awkward. Peter (Cephas) was part of Jesus' inner circle, a beloved disciple, and a prominent, established leader while Paul had been a persecutor of the church before his dramatic salvation. Despite this difficult history, Paul publicly rebuked Peter in Antioch for conduct "not in step with the truth of the gospel."

At first glance, many people would consider Peter's actions a minor issue, but Paul saw them differently. This display of partiality was not a small issue; it was behavior that did not demonstrate the truth of the gospel. In other words, these believers were not living as Christians when divided in the lunch room. Their conduct was anti-gospel.

Paul explained the basis for his rebuke in Galatians 2:14–21, and the heart of his explanation is in verse twenty of the chapter:

> *I have been crucified with Christ. It is no longer I who live, but Christ who lives in me. And the life I now live in the flesh I live by faith in the Son of God, who loved me and gave himself for me.*

This is a well-known verse, and it is part of Paul's explanation for his rebuke in Antioch. It summarizes the "truth of the gospel" that was being neglected in Antioch. This truth is that, if anyone has been born again, they have died and have been given the life of God in the place of their former life.

The good news of the gospel is that God now lives in anyone who has been born again. This is a *truth* and not a *hope*.

The gospel message includes present truths *and* hope for the future. For example, the redemption of our physical bodies is part of the future hope of the gospel.[1] But the presence of Jesus' own life in a born-again person is not a hope; it is a *truth*. Because it is a truth, we can, and should, live out of that life now.

Our outer bodies must still die and be resurrected, but the gift of new life is so real that our inner life *has already died and been resurrected with Jesus' own life*. This is not mystical language; this is our present reality—the truth of the gospel. This truth is so foundational that Paul referred to it numerous times in his letters.[2]

If our old life is dead and we have been given a new life, then anytime we live out of our old life, we are out of step with the gospel and our true condition.

Sins like racism and partiality are normal sins for a fallen human. However, as we have seen, anyone who has been born again is part of a new "species" of humanity like Jesus. Therefore, when we show partiality and discriminate against others on the basis of their old life (and our old life), we act as though we have not become a new human.

---

[1] Romans 8:23; 1 Corinthians 15:12–14, 20–24, 47–49; 1 John 3:2.

[2] Romans 6:6; Galatians 2:20; Colossians 2:20; 2 Timothy 2:11

In another letter, Paul called this kind of partiality behaving like "mere men"[3] because, if you have been born again, you are no longer a "mere human." You are a God-infused human—a completely new kind of creature.

Being "crucified [dead] in Christ" and living out His life is directly connected to how we live with each other, which means racial harmony, unity, and reconciliation are much bigger issues than most people realize. When we live out His life as a new people, we reveal the mystery of Christ, and we confront the powers with the wisdom of God.[4] Therefore, the powers make war on the revelation of Jesus by promoting divisions and stirring racial tension so we will live like "mere men."

In Antioch, Peter and the others were not behaving as a new species of humanity when they prioritized their ethnic distinctions over their new identity in Jesus. This kind of behavior is typical for "mere men," but when we act like "mere men," we behave as though we do not have the new life we have already been given.

The partiality Paul addressed in Antioch is a typical human condition in this age; therefore, only a resurrected humanity with a life not of this age can fulfill John 17.

This leads us to the heart of Paul's revelation of the truth of the gospel. When you are born again, your old person dies in Christ, and you are given a new, divine life *now*. This can be difficult to understand because we do not have our new bodies yet. Our bodies must die so we can receive new bodies when Jesus returns,[5] but Paul understood something spectacular: Our inner man can be resurrected now. If we are in Jesus, our inner man has *already* died, and we have *already* been given our new life. What will happen to our bodies at Jesus' return happens to our inner man now when we receive the Spirit.

A Christian is not a "mere human." A Christian is a person who can live the life of the age to come now. And that's the very life that will come in fullness when Jesus returns.

---

[3] 1 Corinthians 3:3–4.

[4] Ephesians 3:10.

[5] Romans 8:29; 1 Corinthians 15:49; 2 Corinthians 3:18; 4:10–11; 1 John 3:2.

A born-again believer is a present demonstration of a future reality. We do not yet possess the fullness of the age to come because our bodies have not been transformed, but what we possess is real and substantial, and it bears witness to the greater glory that is coming. This expression of Jesus' life is so substantial the church will be the undeniable, living evidence in the darkest moment of history that Jesus exists.

Peter described our calling in Acts 5:

And we are witnesses to these things, and so is the Holy Spirit, whom God has given to those who obey him. (v. 32)

Because the disciples had seen Jesus alive and resurrected, they could give a first-hand account of the message they proclaimed. But they were not the only witnesses. The Holy Spirit is also a living witness that Jesus exists and has been given to *all* those who obey God. The living evidence (witness) that Jesus is alive lives in you if you have been born again, and it enables you to take up the apostles' task. Though you live nearly two thousand years after Jesus' ascension, you are an undeniable witness that Jesus is fully alive just as the apostles were.

Discovering What You Already Possess

The truth that our inner man has already died and we have been given the power of the age to come now profoundly affects the way we view discipleship. We think of the Christian life as a process of receiving new things because of the way we experience life, but our experience can easily obscure our reality. When you were born again, you were given God's own life, and you possess everything in Him.

Discipleship is not a process of receiving new things. It is a process of discovering what you already possess in Jesus.[6]

Peter wrote about this truth in his second letter:

May grace and peace be multiplied to you in the knowledge of God and of Jesus our Lord. His divine power has granted to us all things that pertain to life and godliness, through the knowledge of him who called us to his own glory and excellence, by which he has granted to us his precious and very great promises, so that through them you may become partakers

---

[6] 1 Corinthians 2:10–12.

of the divine nature, having escaped from the corruption that is in the world because of sinful desire. For this very reason, make every effort to supplement your faith with virtue, and virtue with knowledge, and knowledge with self-control, and self-control with steadfastness, and steadfastness with godliness, and godliness with brotherly affection, and brotherly affection with love. For if these qualities are yours and are increasing, they keep you from being ineffective or unfruitful in the knowledge of our Lord Jesus Christ. (1:2–8)

Peter's exhortation helps us grasp the truth of the gospel:

- Grace and peace are multiplied to us in the knowledge of who Jesus is. We experience the joy of life in Jesus by knowing Him.

- Jesus divine power has given us all things that pertain to life and godliness, and our knowledge of Him enables us to "partake" of the divine nature (live like God) and escape the world's corruption.

- We have a completely new life in Jesus, and when we know what we have in Jesus, it empowers us to live differently and begin to live like Him. Our knowledge of Jesus, and who He is in us, will enable us to express new virtues.

Peter had a moment of failure in Antioch, but that failure was redemptive in his life. As a mature apostle, he proclaimed the message that we have been given a new life in Jesus, and we must be a people who demonstrate that life so we are not ineffective or unfruitful in the knowledge of Jesus. Peter's knowledge of Jesus had been "unfruitful" years before in Antioch, but Peter obviously corrected his error.

We need to allow the Holy Spirit to show us the areas where we are "unfruitful" because we do not grasp what has been given to us.

The journey of discipleship is not a process of obtaining some sort of perfection; it is a process of realizing our old inner life really is dead and learning to live out of the new life we already have. In His life, we have been given all things. He is the perfect one, not us. Our life is a process, but growth does not come from self-improvement. Growth comes from discovering and living out of what we have already been given in Jesus. Again, the process of discipleship is learning to live out of what you already possess.

As we have seen, the end-time church will be a mature people who are compatible to Jesus, but it is very important we define maturity correctly. The church will not be stronger, smarter, or more devoted than any other generation. Her people will not be a more "impressive" kind of people.

The end-time church will be a mature people who live *in this age* by what is available in Jesus. His life will become their life. While they will not possess everything that will come in the next age, they will be a substantial and real demonstration of the power of the age to come—a present demonstration of a future reality.

The Christian life is a discovery of what Jesus has done for us. And the mature end-time church will be a people who wholeheartedly live out that gift.

Before Jesus returns, the Father will answer His prayer by producing a people who wholeheartedly live out what is available to them because of the new birth. We have seen glimpses of this over the last two thousand years, but a moment is coming when God will suddenly produce a mature people across the globe. God will be able to produce this people quickly because He does not need to form "better" people. He simply needs a people who live out of the gift they have already been given.

Many people are in distress wanting for God to give them more. This is understandable, but the real issue is we need to discover and experience what we have in Jesus. The answer to our longing to be wholehearted is to explore, encounter, experience, and enjoy His life.

A People from Another Age

We are pilgrims, a people who belong to another age,[7] so discipleship must prepare people to live according to another world and another age. We are a people who confront the system of this age by living according to another age, and we must evaluate our discipleship accordingly. If we are preparing people to succeed according to the culture of this age, we are not discipling them.

We can evaluate our depth of discipleship by asking: Are our people being prepared to live in the age to come, *and* are they living in this age as people of the next age? As we have seen, the primary evidence that Jesus exists is a people who are like Him. When we live

---

[7]Hebrews 11:13; 1 Peter 2:11.

according to the age to come, we become a witness of the reality of that age. If we live our lives according to the culture of this age, our lifestyles deny the truths we claim to believe. We may really be saved, but we are not the witness Jesus prayed for.

A PEOPLE WHO PREPARE THE WAY

Before Jesus appeared the first time, a man named John the Baptist prepared the way for Him. One of the most unusual aspects of John's life was being filled with the Spirit while he was still in his mother's womb.[8] This infilling was a unique gift and a powerful preview of what was coming.

John did not have the fullness of what was coming on the day of Pentecost, but he had a substantial, demonstrable deposit of what was coming *before* it came. Accordingly, when Jesus spoke about John, He did not ask the people who they went to *hear* but who they went to *see* in the wilderness.[9]

John prepared the way for Jesus, and his life demonstrated in part something that would come in fullness when Jesus appeared.

As we have seen, the Lord is preparing a mature, global church that will partner with God to prepare the way for Jesus to return. In many ways, John's ministry before Jesus' first coming is a foreshadowing of the church's preparation for Jesus' second coming. The end-time church will be a corporate John the Baptist throughout the nations, preparing the people of the earth for the return of Jesus.

John emerged suddenly just before Jesus' ministry as one of the greatest men of all history,[10] and the mature end-time church also will seem to emerge suddenly just before Jesus returns. Many people are discouraged by the compromise they perceive in the church, but we must form our opinions about God's people from Bible verses. God is going to shock and amaze the world and even the powers and principalities by bringing His people to maturity before Jesus returns. God is going to form a beautiful, mature people who resemble His Son and become the glorious answer to His Son's prayer.

---

[8] Luke 1:15.

[9] Matthew 11:7–9.

[10] Matthew 11:11; Luke 7:28.

We must not be discouraged. We must put more confidence in Bible verses than what we perceive with our physical eyes.

Just as John demonstrated a measure of the power of what was coming, so also the end-time church will be a demonstration of what is coming. We will not have the fullness of what will come after Jesus returns, but the end-time church will be an undeniable and visible foreshadowing of the glory that will come after Jesus appears again.

As a Spirit-filled man, John pointed to Jesus to such an extent that John was asked if he was the promised Messiah.[11] In the same way, the return of Jesus will be preceded by the maturity of the church.

Like John, the end-time church will be an undeniable witness to what is coming.

For nearly two thousand years, the church has been a people who point to the age to come and the return of the King. As the King and the next age come closer, this assignment will intensify dramatically. We have not received everything we will receive,[12] but what we have is substantial enough to make us witnesses of the future. John was a witness of the glory that would accompany Jesus before Jesus appeared, and the end-time church will also be a witness of the glory that will accompany Jesus' return before He appears. Like John, we will bear witness with our words *and* our lives to what is coming.

We must not be discouraged by our own opinions or the opinions of others about the church. The future of the church is secure. We want to be a people laboring with confidence in the church's future regardless of what we see.

Are you discipling people in confidence that this witness is coming?

---

[11] Luke 3:15; John 1:19–20; 3:28.

[12] 2 Corinthians 1:22; Ephesians 1:13–14; 4:30.

DO WE SHARE GOD'S ZEAL?

Do you share God's zeal for His Son and His Son's people? If you do, you will give your life to make disciples.

Nearly all believers will say discipleship is important and the main task Jesus has given us, but tragically very few people prioritize discipleship in their daily lives. Many believers do not pursue personal discipleship and do not actively disciple others. However, this will change because Jesus wants a discipled people, and we are a critical part of His plan.

Lack of interest in discipleship is an indicator we have little vision for what God wants.

Far more is at stake in our churches, small groups, and daily discipleship than we realize. Jesus will not return until a people have come to maturity and become a public, undeniable witness (demonstration) of who He is. We have seen glimpses of this witness throughout history, but something is coming far beyond what we have imagined. When we consider what Jesus said about His church, the glory of the mature, end-time church is perhaps the most overlooked theme of the end times.

We cannot control the time of Jesus' return, but we must decide whether or not we will engage in the process that will give Him His reward and set the stage for His coming.

A friend said it best:

> The church is a matter of eschatological urgency, because Jesus will not return until the church is mature. If you want Jesus to return, it is a tangible way to hasten the return of Jesus.[1]

---

[1] Andrew Tam stated this in a personal conversation.

With that in mind, we must ask: *Is it possible our lack of interest in the church is holding back the return of Jesus?*

Much of the body *is* vibrantly engaged in discipleship, but right now there are still significant parts of the body that have a tragic lack of engagement in discipleship. Jesus asked for a people, and the Father will answer that request. If the Scripture is not enough to provoke us to actively engage in discipleship, God will change our situation to produce the kind of discipleship necessary to give Jesus what He wants.

In the days ahead, God is going to release radical shifts across the earth. These shifts will bring dramatic changes to economies, nations, and societies. However, these shifts will not primarily be about the nations. These shifts will be about the church because God is not leading history to affect the nations. He is leading history to produce a church. He will not hesitate to "disrupt" the world in ways we cannot imagine to produce the church He wants.

He will do whatever is necessary to shape a church that is deeply committed to discipleship.

The greatest gift you can give God is allowing Him to lead your life and make you like Jesus. The second greatest gift you can give Him is to actively work with Him to see a people formed into His image.

Many people act as though discipleship is an optional activity, but it is not. Discipleship is the way Jesus receives His reward, and it requires our engagement. If we do not actively obey Jesus, we rob Jesus of His reward because the Father's plan to reward Jesus requires the partnership and active involvement of His people.

If you are discipling, no matter how "small" it seems, you are advancing God's plan. If you are not discipling, you are hindering God's plan.

REFOCUSING MISSIONS

When we consider the immense task of world missions (nearly two billion people have not heard the gospel yet), the desire God has for all people to hear the gospel (God wants a remnant from every people in His people[2]), and the unique moment we live in (we could potentially

---

[2]Genesis 12:3; 28:14; Deuteronomy 32:21; Psalm 22:27; Isaiah 24:14–16; 42:10–12; 49:6; 56:6–7; 60:1–3; 65:1; Jeremiah 16:19–21; Amos 9:11–12; Zechariah 2:11; 14:16; Malachi 1:11; Matthew 24:14; 28:19; Acts 1:6–8; Romans 15:9; Revelation 5:9; 7:9.

evangelize all peoples within a generation[3]), we are tempted to engage in mass evangelism and try to find faster ways to get the "task" of world missions done.

Yet, Jesus' methodology was very different from ours. He left us with a commission designed to fulfill the task of world missions:

Go therefore and make disciples of all nations. (Matthew 28:19)

The Lord gives certain individuals gifts for large-scale evangelism, but that does not exempt us from fully obeying what Jesus said. Evangelism is necessary and important, but it cannot fulfill the mission we have been given. The mission must be fulfilled by active discipleship. We must reorient our thinking. We have tried to industrialize world missions, but this does not work. God gives grace for large-scale evangelism, but that must be followed by the difficult, daily work of discipleship. This labor of life and love is at the heart of the mission.

Furthermore, the task of discipleship was given to the entire church. It is not just for pastors or vocational ministers. God never intended the church to have a few paid "professional" people who disciple and a large body who leaves the task to these "professionals." God gives individuals leadership gifts so that the entire body can engage in discipleship.[4]

Depending on where you live, you now have more leisure time than any generation in history,[5] and you must ask, "Why has God given me so much free time?" We have far more free time than the apostles, the church fathers, or any of the well-known saints in history. It is historic. Did God design this moment of history so we could experience more comfort, media, hobbies, recreation, or entertainment than any other generation, or is He after something else?

---

[3]This is a general assumption of many missiologists based on the data currently known, but this would require significant effort.

[4]Ephesians 4:11–13.

[5]Brian Harris, "Sorry, I've no time. Really?" https://brianharrisauthor.com/sorry-ive-no-time-really/, accessed November 6, 2020.

God has given us more free time than any other generation (and we will have even more in the days ahead) so we can immerse ourselves into discipleship more than any other generation to see the glorious end-time church emerge.

He has also given us far more access to the Bible and resources than any generation in history. We can easily and freely access incredible tools to help us understand the message of the Bible. All of this is being orchestrated by God for an unprecedented end-time wave of discipleship that happens with the involvement of the entire church.

God has given us profound gifts: unprecedented time and resources that enable us to disciple a people, so Jesus gets what He wants.

You may struggle with discouragement because of what you have experienced in your own life or your local church. Perhaps others did not disciple you well, or you have tried to invest in others who were apathetic. Your frustration is understandable because Jesus also faced apathy and lack of interest,[6] but you must put more confidence in Bible verses than what you have experienced or what you perceive.

I guarantee in the age to come we will all wish we had put more confidence in what God has said than what we experienced.

No one expected God to become a man and reveal Himself the way He did. In the same way, we do not fully grasp God's plan to reveal His Son in a people at the end of the age. If we truly understand that plan, we will engage in His plan with newfound confidence. The apostles were fully convinced the Father would answer Jesus' prayer and give them power by the Spirit to play their part in preparing a people. That confidence enabled them to endure all kinds of challenges and continue day by day to give their lives for the sake of a people.

This age will not end until Jesus' prayer is answered. The Father is the only one who can answer the prayer, but we play a part in giving Jesus the reward He wants and deserves. This people will emerge in the most difficult moment of history,[7] which raises another question: *Do we disciple and prepare people to endure the greatest crisis of all time?*

This is not an issue of trying to predict the precise timing of the end-time trouble. When Jesus described the end-time trouble in Matthew 24–25, He warned that the end-time trouble will come

---

[6]Matthew 23:37; John 1:11; 3:19; 5:39–40; 8:45–46.

[7]Jeremiah 30:7; Daniel 12:1; Matthew 24:21; Revelation 12:11.

suddenly, it will be a surprise, and when it comes, it will be too late to prepare. His parables all carry a consistent message: We must be prepared for the end-time trouble at any time. Preparing the church for the end-time crisis was a key part of Jesus' discipleship methodology.

Jesus instructed us to prepare ourselves and others for the end-time crisis.

It is important we prepare biblically because some have responded to Jesus' teaching in unbiblical ways, which include trying to predict the date of Jesus' return, becoming immersed in unhelpful speculation, and neglecting active involvement in the life of the church. We must avoid unbiblical and unhelpful responses to Jesus' teaching, but we must not neglect the response Jesus commanded.

We *must* disciple a people who survive the end-time crisis to obey Jesus. If we do it correctly, it will produce a people who are prepared to resist evil men and set their hope and affection on Jesus and His return. A people discipled this way will be able to endure suffering and resist the seduction of comfort.

How Do We Do It?

How do we disciple with a biblical paradigm?

First, we must live with wisdom that comes from insight into God's purpose for this age:

- He wants to reveal Himself in the person of Jesus.
- He wants to form a people who become like Him.

This wisdom produces a paradigm of discipleship that will enable the church to become what Jesus wants her to be. According to the New Testament, that paradigm can be summarized as "Discipleship begins with beholding." We must intentionally design our practices of discipleship so we behold Jesus and become like Him, because discipleship is not primarily about information; it is about imitation.

How do we live a life of wisdom? How do we disciple with a New Testament paradigm in mind? Those questions are explored in the companion volume, *Discipleship Begins with Beholding*.

Acknowledgments

Thank you to my wife whose labor and sacrifice make it possible for us to engage in the task the Lord has given us.

Thank you to the entire family for enduring the process that has produced the message in this book.

Thank you to all those who have invested effort in my own discipleship. I owe you more than I can ever pay.

Thank you to Jason Chua and the Burning Hearts community. Our time spent studying Jesus' desire for a people shaped this book tremendously.

Thank you to Edie Mourey for your work on this manuscript.

Thank you to the prayer team who has faithfully prayed for this book. The Lord released grace in response to your petitions.

www.ingramcontent.com/pod-product-compliance
Lightning Source LLC
Chambersburg PA
CBHW071342080526
44587CB00017B/2936